Elbert Hubbard

Little Journeys to the Homes of American Authors

Elbert Hubbard

Little Journeys to the Homes of American Authors

ISBN/EAN: 9783744755481

Printed in Europe, USA, Canada, Australia, Japan

Cover: Foto ©Andreas Hilbeck / pixelio.de

More available books at **www.hansebooks.com**

Little

Journeys

To the Homes of American Authors

Published in New York
and London by
G. P. Putnam's Sons

PUBLISHERS' NOTE.

In 1853, the late G. P. Putnam published, under the title of *Homes of American Authors*, a collection of papers which had been written for this work by a group of the younger writers of the day, and which were devoted to studies and descriptions of the homes and of the work of certain representative American authors of the time. The plan of the series originated, we understand, with the publisher, while it is probable that its editorial direction rested either with Henry T. Tuckerman or Charles F. Briggs ("Harry Franco"), who was at the time editor of *Putnam's Monthly*. Among the contributors were several writers whose work has since made for itself a place in the enduring literature of the century. Of these contributors (a list of whom will be found on the preceding page) but two, Parke Godwin and Edward Everett Hale, are still (December, 1895) surviving.

The successors of G. P. Putnam have thought that the generation which has grown up since the first publication of this book would be interested in reading these literary studies of half a century back. It has, therefore, been decided to reprint the papers as the second group of the series of *Little Journeys*, the publication of which has been initiated with the twelve papers of Mr. Elbert Hubbard issued in 1895.

These papers of 1853 are printed as originally written for Mr. Putnam's volume, and as a matter of justice to authors who, like Mr. Curtis and Mr. Godwin, have since written more comprehensively on the same subjects, the date of the original publication has in each case been specified. There is a certain literary interest in having again before us the point of view of these writers of 1853, even although in certain cases their final conclusions may have been somewhat modified, or their maturer literary judgment may have arrived at some different form of literary expression.

CONTENTS

ILLUSTRATIONS

Illustrations

EMERSON

His goodness seems better than our goodness,
his nature finer, his temptations less. Everything that is his,—his name, his form, his dress,
books, and instruments,—fancy enhances.

Essay on Friendship.

FOREWORD

They are gone—writer and subject—gone. The dust of Emerson rests in "Sleepy Hollow": a great unhewn bowlder marks the spot. He died in 1882; Curtis followed ten years later. But their works live after them: for beautiful lives and great thoughts endure. They make that sweet minor chord in the choir invisible, whose music is the gladness of the world. Curtis was in his twenty-ninth year when he wrote this sketch; Emerson was fifty—his fame secure. No living writer, no matter how richly gifted, could write so precious a monograph as this on the same theme; 't would lack that quaint old flavor and fragrance, as of lavender and thyme.

E. H.

HOME OF EMERSON, Concord, Mass.

EMERSON.

BY GEORGE WILLIAM CURTIS.*

THE village of Concord, Massachusetts, lies an hour's ride from Boston. It is one of those quiet New England towns whose few white houses, grouped upon the plain, make but a slight impression upon the mind of the busy traveller hurrying to or from the city. As the conductor calls "Concord!" the tourist has scarcely time to recall "Concord, Lexington, and Bunker Hill," before the place has vanished, and he is darting through woods and fields as solitary as those he has just left in New

* Written in 1853 for Putnam's *Homes of American Authors.*

5

Hampshire. Yet, as it vanishes, he may chance to see two or three spires, and as they rush behind the trees his eyes fall upon a gleaming sheet of water. It is Walden Pond,—or Walden Water, as Orphic Alcott used to call it,—whose virgin seclusion was a just image of that of the little village until one afternoon, some half-dozen or more years since, a shriek, sharper than any that had rung from Walden woods since the last war-whoop of the last Indians of Musketaquid, announced to astonished Concord, drowsing in the river meadows, that the nineteenth century had overtaken it. Yet long before the material force of the age bound the town to the rest of the world, the spiritual force of a single mind in it had attracted attention to it, and made its lonely plains as dear to many widely-scattered minds as the groves of the Academy or the vineyards of Vaucluse.

Except in causing the erection of the railway buildings and several dwellings near it, steam has not much changed

Concord. It is yet one of the quiet country towns whose charm is incredible to all but those who by loving it have found it worthy of love. The shire-town of the great agricultural county of Middlesex, it is not disturbed by the feverish throb of factories, nor by any roar of inexorable toil but the few puffs of the locomotive. One day, during the autumn, it is thronged by the neighboring farmers, who hold their high festival—the annual cattle-show—there. But the calm tenor of Concord life is not varied even on that day by anything more exciting than fat oxen and the cud-chewing eloquence of the agricultural dinner. The population of the region is composed of sturdy, sterling men, worthy representatives of the ancestors who sowed along the Concord shores, with their seed-corn and rye, the germs of a prodigious national greatness. At intervals every day the rattle, roar, and whistle of the swift shuttle darting to and from the metropolitan heart of New England, weaving prosperity upon the land, remind those farmers in their silent fields that the great world yet wags and wrestles. And the farmer-boy, sweeping with flashing scythe through the river meadows, whose coarse grass glitters, apt for mowing, in the early June morning, pauses as the whistle dies into the distance, and, wiping his brow and whetting his blade anew, questions the country-smitten citizen, the amateur farmer struggling with imperfect stroke behind him of the mystic romance of city life.

The sluggish repose of the little river images the farmer-boy's life. He bullies his oxen and trembles at the locomotive. His wonder and fancy stretch toward the great world beyond the barn-yard and the village church, as the torpid stream tends toward the ocean. The river, in fact, seems the thread upon which all the beads of that rustic life are strung,— the clew to its tranquil character. If it were an impetuous stream, dashing along as if it claimed and required the career to

which every American river is entitled,
—a career it would have. Wheels, factories, shops, traders, factory-girls, boards
of directors, dreary white lines of boarding-houses, all the signs that indicate the
spirit of the age, and of the American
age, would arise upon its margin. Some
shaven magician from State Street would
run up by rail, and, from proposals, maps,
schedules of stock, etc., educe a spacious
factory as easily as Aladdin's palace arose
from nothing. Instead of a dreaming,
pastoral poet of a village, Concord would
be a rushing, whirling, bustling manu-
facturer of a town, like its thrifty neighbor Lowell. Many a fine equipage,
flashing along city ways; many an
Elizabethan-Gothic-Grecian rural retreat,
in which State Street woos Pan and grows
Arcadian in summer, would be reduced,
in the last analysis, to the Concord mills.
Yet if these broad river meadows grew
factories instead of corn, they might, perhaps, lack another harvest, of which the
poet's thought is the sickle.

One harvest from your field
  Homeward brought the oxen strong,
Another crop your acres yield,
  Which I gather in a song,

sings Emerson; and again, as the afternoon light strikes pensive across his
memory, as over the fields below him,

Knows he who tills this lonely field,
  To reap its scanty corn,
What mystic crops his acres yield
  At midnight and at morn?

The Concord River—upon whose winding shores the town has scattered its few
houses, as if, loitering over the plain
some fervent day, it had fallen asleep
obedient to the slumberous spell, and
had not since awakened—is a languid,
shallow stream, that loiters through
broad meadows, which fringe it with
rushes and long grasses. Its sluggish
current scarcely moves the autumn leaves
showered upon it by a few maples that
lean over the Assabeth—as one of its
branches is named. Yellow lily-buds
and leathery lily-pads tessellate its surface, and the white water-lilies—pale,

proud ladies of Shalott—bare their bosoms to the sun in the seclusion of its
distant reaches. Clustering vines of wild
grape hang its wooded shores with a
tapestry of the South and the Rhine.
The pickerel-weed marks with blue
spikes of flowers the points where small
tributary brooks flow in, and along the
dusky winding of those brooks, cardinal-
flowers with a scarlet splendor paint the
Tropics upon New England's green. All
summer long, from founts unknown, in
the upper counties, from some anonymous pond, or wooded hillside moist with
springs, steals the gentle river through
the plain, spreading at one point above
the town into a little lake, called by the
farmers "Fairhaven Bay," as if all its
lesser names must share the sunny significance of Concord. Then, shrinking
again, alarmed at its own boldness, it
dreams on toward the Merrimac and the
sea.

The absence of factories has already
implied its shallowness and slowness. In

truth it is a very slow river, belonging
much more to the Indian than to the
Yankee; so much so, indeed, that until
a very few years there was an annual
visit to its shores from a few sad heirs of
its old masters, who pitched a group of
tents in the meadows, and wove their
tidy baskets and strung their beads in
unsmiling silence. It was the same
thing that I saw in Jerusalem among
the Jews. Every Friday they repair to
the remains of the old Temple wall, and
pray and wail, kneeling upon the pave-
ment and kissing the stones. But that
passionate Oriental regret was not more
impressive than this silent homage of a
waning race, who, as they beheld the
unchanged river, knew that, unlike it,
the last drops of their existence were
gradually flowing away, and that for their
tribes there shall be no ingathering.

So shallow is the stream that the amateur Corydons who embark at morning
to explore its remoter shores will not
infrequently, in midsummer, find their

boat as suddenly tranquil and motionless as the river, having placidly grounded upon its oozy bottom. Or, returning at evening, they may lean over the edge as they lie at length in the boat, and float with the almost imperceptible current, brushing the tips of the long water-grass and reeds below them in the stream—a river jungle, in which lurk pickerel and trout—with the sensation of a bird drifting upon soft evening air over the tree-tops. No available or profitable craft navigate these waters, and animated gentlemen from the city, who run up for "a mouthful of fresh air," cannot possibly detect the final cause of such a river. Yet the dreaming idler has place on maps and a name in history.

Near the town it is crossed by three or four bridges. One is a massive structure to help the railroad over. The stern, strong pile readily betrays that it is part of good, solid stock owned in the right quarter. Close by it is a little arched stone bridge, auxiliary to a great road

leading to some vague region of the
world called Acton upon guideposts and
on maps. Just beyond these bridges the
river bends, and forgets the railroad, but
is grateful to the graceful arch of the
little stone bridge for making its curve
more picturesque; and, as it muses toward
the Old Manse, listlessly brushing the
lilies, it wonders if Ellery Channing, who
lives beyond, upon a hillside sloping to
the shore, wrote his poem of *The Bridge*
to that particular one. There are two or
three wooden bridges also, always com-
bining well with the landscape, always
making and suggesting pictures.

The Concord, as I said, has a name in
history. Near one of the wooden bridges
you turn aside from the main road, close
by the " Old Manse,"—whose mosses of
mystic hue were gathered by Hawthorne,
who lived there for three years,—and a
few steps bring you to the river, and to a
small monument upon its brink. It is
a narrow, grassy way; not a field nor a
meadow, but of that shape and charac-

ter which would perplex the animated stranger from the city, who would see, also, its unfitness for a building-lot. The narrow, grassy way is the old road which, in the month of April, 1775, led to a bridge that crossed the stream at this spot. And upon the river's margin, upon the bridge and the shore beyond, took place the sharp struggle between the Middlesex farmers and the scarlet British soldiers, known in tradition as " The Concord fight."

The small monument records the day and the event. When it was erected, Emerson wrote the following hymn for the ceremony :

APRIL 19, 1836.

By the rude bridge that arched the flood,
  Their flag to April's breeze unfurled,
Here once the embattled farmers stood,
  And fired the shot heard round the world.

The foe long since in silence slept ;
  Alike the conqueror silent sleeps ;
And Time the ruined bridge has swept
  Down the dark stream that seaward creeps.

On this green bank, by this soft stream,
  We see to-day a votive stone,
That memory may their deed redeem,
  When, like our sires, our sons are gone.

Spirit that made these heroes dare
  To die, or leave their children free,
Bid Time and Nature gently spare
  The shaft we raise to them and Thee.

Close under the rough stone wall at the left, which separates it from the grassy orchard of the Manse, is a small mound of turf and a broken stone. Grave and headstone shrink from sight amid the grass and under the wall, but they mark the earthly bed of the first victims of that first fight. A few large trees overhang the ground, which Hawthorne thinks have been planted since that day, and he says that in the river he has seen mossy timbers of the old bridge, and on the farther bank, half-hidden, the crumbling stone abutments that supported it. In an old house upon the main road, nearly opposite the entrance to this grassy way, I knew a hale old woman who well remembered the gay advance of the flashing soldiers, the terrible ring and crack of firearms, and the panic-stricken retreat of the regulars, blackened and bloody. But the placid river has long since overborne it all. The alarm, the struggle, the retreat, are swallowed up in its supreme tranquillity. The summers of more than seventy years have obliterated every trace of the road with thick grass, which seeks to bury the graves as earth buried the victims.

Let the sweet ministry of summer avail. Let its mild iteration even sap the monument and conceal its stones as it hides the abutment in foliage ; for, still on the sunny slopes, white with the May blossoming of apple-orchards, and in the broad fields, golden to the marge of the river, and tilled in security and peace, survives the imperishable remembrance of that day and its results.

The river is thus the main feature of the Concord landscape. It is surrounded by a wide plain, from which rise only three or four low hills. One is a wooded cliff over Fairhaven Bay, a mile from the town ; one separates the main river from the Assabeth ; and just beyond the battle-ground another rises, rich with orchards, to a fine wood which crowns its summit. The river meadows blend with broad, lonely fields. A wide horizon, like that of the prairie or the sea, is the grand charm of Concord. At night the stars are seen from the roads crossing the plain, as from a ship at sea. The landscape would be called tame by those who think no scenery grand but that of mountains or the sea-coast. But the wide solitude of that region is not so accounted by those who live there. To them it is rich and suggestive, as Emerson shows in the *Essay on Nature :* " My house stands in low land, with limited outlook, and on the skirt of the village. But I go with my friend to the shore of our little river, and with one stroke of the paddle I leave the village politics and personalities—yes, and the world of villages and personalities—behind, and pass into a delicate realm of sunset and moonlight, too bright almost for spotted man to enter without novitiate and probation. We penetrate bodily this incredible beauty ; we dip our hands in this painted element ; our eyes are bathed in these lights and forms. A holiday, a royal revel, the proudest, most heart-rejoicing festival that valor and beauty, power and taste ever decked and enjoyed, establishes itself upon the instant. . . . In every landscape the point of astonishment is the meeting of the sky and the earth, and that is seen from the first hillock, as well as from the top of the Alleghanies. The stars stoop down over the brownest, homeliest common, with all the spiritual magnificence which they shed on the Campagna or on the marble deserts of Egypt.''

He is speaking here, of course, of the spiritual excitement of beauty, which crops up everywhere in Nature, like gold in a rich region ; but the quality of the imagery indicates the character of the scenery in which the essay was written.

Concord is too far from Boston to rival in garden cultivation its neighbors, West Cambridge, Lexington, and Waltham; nor can it boast, with Brookline, Dorchester, and Cambridge, the handsome summer homes of city wealth. But it surpasses them all, perhaps, in a genuine country freshness and feeling derived from its loneliness. If not touched by city elegance, neither is it infected by city meretriciousness—it is sweet, wholesome country. By climbing one of the hills, your eye sweeps a wide, wide landscape, until it rests upon graceful Wachuset, or, farther and mistier, Monadnoc, the lofty outpost of New Hampshire hills. Level scenery is not tame. The ocean, the prairie, the desert are not tame, although of monotonous surface. The gentle undulations which mark certain scenes,—a rippling landscape, in which all sense of space, of breadth, and of height is lost,—that is tame. It may be made beautiful by exquisite cultivation, as it often is in England and on parts of the Hudson shores, but it is, at best, rather pleasing than inspiring. For a permanent view the eye craves large and simple forms, as the body requires plain food for its best nourishment.

The town of Concord is built mainly upon one side of the river. In its centre is a large open square shaded by fine elms. A white wooden church, in the most classical style of Yankee-Greek, stands upon the square. At the Court-House, in the days when I knew Concord, many conventions were held for humane as well as political objects. One summer day I especially remember, when I did not envy Athens its Forum, for Emerson and William Ellery Channing spoke. In the speech of both burned the sacred fire of eloquence, but in Emerson it was light, and in Channing, heat.

From this square diverge four roads, like highways from a forum. One leads by the Court-House and under stately sycamores to the Old Manse and the battle-ground, another goes directly to the river, and a third is the main avenue of the town. After passing the shops this third divides, and one branch forms a fair and noble street, spacious, and loftily arched with elms, the houses standing liberally apart, each with its garden-plot in front. The fourth avenue is the old Boston road, also dividing, at the edge of the village, into the direct route to the metropolis and the Lexington turnpike.

The house of Mr. Emerson stands opposite this junction. It is a plain, square, white dwelling-house, yet it has a city air, and could not be mistaken for a farm-house. A quiet merchant, you would say, unostentatious and simple, has here hidden himself from town. But a thick grove of pine and fir trees, almost brushing the two windows upon the right of the door, and occupying the space between them and the road, suggests at least a peculiar taste in the retired merchant, or hints the possibility that he may have sold his place to a poet or philosopher,—or to some old East India sea-captain, perhaps, who cannot sleep without the sound of waves, and so plants pines to rustle, surf-like, against his chamber-window.

The fact, strangely enough, partly supports your theory. In the year 1828 Mr. C. Coolidge, a brother of J. Templeman Coolidge, a merchant of repute in Boston, and grandson of Joseph Coolidge, a patriarchal denizen of Bowdoin Square in that city, came to Concord and built this house. Gratefully remembering the lofty horse-chestnuts which shaded the city square, and which, perhaps, first inspired him with the wish to be a nearer neighbor of woods and fields, he planted a row of them along his lot, which this year ripen their twenty-fifth harvest. With the liberal hospitality of a New England merchant, he did not forget the spacious cellars of the city, and, as Mr. Emerson writes, " he built the only good cellar that had then been built in Concord."

Mr. Emerson bought the house in the year 1835. He found it a plain, convenient, and thoroughly-built country residence. An amiable neighbor of Mr. Coolidge had placed a miserable old barn irregularly upon the edge of that gentleman's lot, which, for the sake of comeliness, he was forced to buy and set straight and smooth into a decent dependence of the mansion-house. The estate, upon passing into Mr. Emerson's hands, comprised the house, barn, and two acres of land. He enlarged the house and barn, and the two acres have grown to nine. Our author is no farmer, except as every country gentleman is, yet the kindly slope from the rear of the house to a little brook, which, passing to the calm Concord beyond, washes the edge of his land, yields him at least occasional beans and peas ; or some friend, agriculturally enthusiastic, and an original Brook Farmer, experiments with guano in the garden, and produces melons and other vines with a success that relieves Brook Farm from every slur of inadequate practical genius. Mr. Emerson has shaded his originally bare land with trees, and counts near a hundred apple and pear trees in his orchard. The whole estate is quite level, inclining only toward the little brook, and is well watered and convenient.

The Orphic Alcott,—or Plato Skimpole, as Margaret Fuller called him,—well-known in the transcendental history of New England, designed and with his own hands erected a summer-house, which gracefully adorns the lawn, if I may so call the smooth grass-plot at the side of the house. Unhappily, this edifice promises no long duration, not being "technically based and pointed." This is not a strange, although a disagreeable fact to Mr. Emerson, who has been always the most faithful and appreciating of the lovers of Mr. Alcott. It is natural that the Orphic Alcott should build graceful summer-houses. There are even people who declare that he has covered the pleasant but somewhat misty lawns of ethical speculation with a thousand such edifices, which need only to be a little more "technically based and pointed" to be quite perfect. At present, they whisper, the wind blows clean through them, and no figures of flesh and blood are ever seen there, but only pallid phantoms with large, calm eyes, eating uncooked grain out of baskets, and discoursing in a sublime shibboleth of which mortals have no key. But how could Plato Skimpole, who goes down to Hingham on the sea, in a New England January, clad only in a suit of linen, hope to build immortal summer-houses?

Mr. Emerson's library is the room at the right of the door upon entering the house. It is a simple square room, not walled with books like the den of a literary grub, nor merely elegant like the ornamental retreat of a dilettante. The books are arranged upon plain shelves, not in architectural bookcases, and the room is hung with a few choice engravings of the greatest men. There was a fair copy of Michael Angelo's *Fates*, which, properly enough, imparted that grave serenity to the ornament of the room which is always apparent in what is written there. It is the study of a scholar. All our author's published writings, the essays, orations, and poems, date from this room, as much as they date from any place or moment. The villagers, indeed, fancy their philosophic neighbor affected by the novelist James's constancy of composition. They relate, with wide eyes, that he has a huge manuscript book, in which he incessantly records the ends of thoughts, bits of observation and experience, and facts of all kinds,—a kind of intellectual and scientific rag-bag, into which all shreds and remnants of conversations and reminiscences of wayside reveries are incontinently thrust. This work goes on, they aver, day and night; and when he travels, the rag-bag travels too, and grows more plethoric with each mile of the journey. And a story, which will one day be a tradition, is perpetuated, that one night, before his wife had become completely accustomed to his habits, she awoke suddenly, and hearing him groping about the room, inquired anxously :

"My dear, are you ill ? "

"No, my love, only an idea."

The library is not only the study of a scholar, it is the bower of a poet. The pines lean against the windows, and to the student deeply sunk in learned lore, or soaring upon the daring speculations of an intrepid philosophy, they whisper a secret beyond that of the philosopher's stone, and sing of the springs of poetry.

The site of the house is not memorable. There is no reasonable ground to suppose that so much as an Indian wigwam ever occupied the spot ; nor has Henry Thoreau, a very faithful friend of Mr. Emerson's, and of the woods and waters of his native Concord, ever found an Indian arrowhead upon the premises. Henry's instinct is as sure toward the facts of nature as the witch-hazel toward treasure. If every quiet country town in New England had a son who, with a lore like Selbourne's, and an eye like Buffon's, had watched and studied its landscape and history, and then published the result, as Thoreau has done, in a book as redolent of genuine and perceptive sympathy with nature as a clover-field of honey, New England would seem as poetic and beautiful as Greece. Thoreau lives in a blackberry pasture upon a bank over Walden pond, in a little house of his own building. One pleasant summer afternoon a small party of us helped him raise it,—a bit of life as Arcadian as any at Brook Farm. Elsewhere in the village he turns up arrowheads abundantly, and Hawthorne mentions that Thoreau initiated him into the mystery of finding them. But neither the Indians, nor Nature, nor Thoreau can invest the quiet residence of our author with the dignity, or even the suspicion, of a legend. History stops short in that direction with Charles Coolidge, Esq., and the year 1828.

There is little prospect from the house. Directly opposite, a low bluff overhangs the Boston road and obstructs the view. Upon the other sides the level land stretches away. Toward Lexington it is a broad, half-marshy region, and between the brook behind and the river, good farms lie upon the outskirts of the town. Pilgrims drawn to Concord by the desire of conversing with the man whose written or spoken eloquence has so profoundly charmed them, and who have placed him in some pavilion of fancy, some peculiar residence, find him in no porch of philosophy nor academic grove, but in a plain white house by the wayside, ready to entertain every comer as an ambassador from some remote Cathay of speculation whence the stars are more nearly seen.

But the familiar reader of our author will not be surprised to find the poet

They say
that vegetation
about your
full grown
forest. It is
a fact, the con-
ditions objects,
who cannot
be but seventy
sixty six
the

They say that by electro-magnetism vegetation may be so accelerated, that your sallad shall be grown whilst your fowl is roasting for dinner. It is a symbol of our modern life, the condensation & acceleration of objects. But nothing is gained, nature cannot be cheated. Man's life is but seventy sallads long, grow they swift or grow they slow simply sheltered, and the endless experimenter, with no past at his back, housed without ornament. Such a reader will have felt the Spartan severity of this intellect, and have noticed that the realm of this imagination is rather sculpturesque than pictorial, more Greek than Italian. Therefore he will be pleased to alight at the gate, and hear the breezy welcome of the pines, and the no less cordial salutation of their owner. For if the visitor knows what he is about, he has come to this plain for bracing mountain air. These serious Concord reaches are no vale of Cashmere. Where Plato Skimpole is architect of the summerhouse, you may imagine what is to be expected in the mansion itself. It is always morning within those doors. If you have nothing to say,—if you are really not an envoy from some kingdom or colony of thought, and cannot cast a gem upon the heaped pile,—you had better pass by on the other side. For it is the peculiarity of Emerson's mind to be always on the alert.   He eats no lotus, but forever quaffs the waters which engender immortal thirst.

If the memorabilia of his house could find their proper Xenophon, the want of antecedent arrowheads upon the premises would not prove very disastrous to the interest of the history.   The fame of the philosopher attracts admiring friends and enthusiasts from every quarter, and the scholarly grace and urbane hospitality of the gentleman send them charmed away. Friendly foes, who altogether differ from Emerson, come to break a lance with him upon the level pastures of Concord, with all the cheerful and appreciative zeal of those who longed

> To drink delight of battle with their peers
> Far on the ringing plains of windy Troy.

It is not hazardous to say that the greatest questions of our day and of all days, have been nowhere more amply discussed with more poetic insight or profound conviction than in the comely, square white house upon the edge of the Lexington turnpike. There have even been attempts at something more formal and club-like than the chance conversations of occasional guests, one of which will certainly be nowhere recorded but upon these pages.

It was in the year 1845 that a circle of persons of various ages, and differing very much in everything but sympathy, found themselves in Concord. Toward the end of the autumn Mr. Emerson suggested that they should meet every Monday evening through the winter in his library. "Monsieur Aubepine," "Miles Coverdale," and other phantoms, since generally known as Nathaniel Hawthorne, who then occupied the Old Manse ; the inflexible Henry Thoreau, a scholastic and pastoral Orson, then living among the blackberry pastures of Walden pond ; Plato Skimpole, then sublimely meditating impossible summer-houses in a little house upon the Boston road ; the enthusiastic agriculturist and

Brook Farmer already mentioned, then an inmate of Mr. Emerson's house, who added the genial cultivation of a scholar to the amenities of the natural gentleman ; a sturdy farmer neighbor, who had bravely fought his weary way through inherited embarrassments to the small success of a New England husbandman, and whose faithful wife had seven times merited well of her country ; two city youths, ready for the fragments from the feast of wit and wisdom, and the host himself composed this Club. Ellery Channing, who had that winter harnessed his Pegasus to the *New York Tribune*, was a kind of corresponding member. The news of the world was to be transmitted through his eminently practical genius, as the Club deemed itself competent to take charge of tidings from all other spheres.

I went the first Monday evening, very much as Ixion may have gone to his banquet. The philosophers sat dignified and erect. There was a constrained, but

very amiable, silence, which had the im-
pertinence of a tacit inquiry, seeming to
ask : " Who will now proceed to say the
finest thing that has ever been said ? " It
was quite voluntary and unavoidable,
for the members lacked that fluent social
genius without which a club is impossible.
It was a congress of oracles on the one
hand, and of curious listeners upon the
other. I vaguely remember that the
Orphic Alcott invaded the Sahara of silence with a solemn "saying," to which,
after due pause, the honorable member
for Blackberry Pastures responded by
some keen and graphic observation ; while
the Olympian host, anxious that so much
good material should be spun into something, beamed smiling encouragement
upon all parties.

But the conversation became more and
more staccato. Miles Coverdale, a statue
of night and silence, sat, a little removed,
under a portrait of Dante, gazing imper-
turbably upon the group ; and as he sat
in the shadow, his dark hair and eyes

and suit of sables made him, in that society, the black thread of mystery which he weaves into his stories, while the shifting presence of the Brook Farmer played like heat-lightning around the room.

I recall little else but a grave eating of russet apples by the erect philosophers, and a solemn disappearance into the night. The Club struggled through three Monday evenings. Plato was perpetually putting apples of gold in pictures of silver; for such was the rich ore of his thoughts, coined by the deep melody of his voice. Orson charmed us with the secrets won from his interviews with Pan in the Walden woods—while Emerson, with the zeal of an engineer trying to dam wild waters, sought to bind the wide-flying embroidery of discourse into a web of clear, sweet sense. But still in vain. The oracular sayings were the unalloyed saccharine element; and every chemist knows how much else goes to practical food; how much coarse, rough, woody fibre is essential.

The Club struggled on valiantly, discoursing celestially, eating apples, and disappearing in the dark, until the third evening it vanished altogether. Yet I have since known clubs of fifty times that number, whose collective genius was not more than of either one of the Dii Majores of our Concord coterie. The fault was its too great concentration. It was not relaxation, as a club should be, but tension. Society is a play, a game, a tournament; not a battle. It is the easy grace of undress; not an intellectual, full-dress parade.

I have already hinted this unbending intellectual alacrity of our author. His sport is serious—his humor is earnest. He stands like a sentinel. His look and manner and habit of thought cry; "Who goes there?" and if he does not hear the countersign, he brings the intruder to a halt. It is for this surprising fidelity and integrity that his influence has been so deep, and sure, and permanent, upon the intellectual life of the young men of New

England ; and of Old England, too, where in Manchester there were regular weekly meetings at which his works were read. What he said long ago in his preface to the American edition of Carlyle's *Miscellanies*, that they were papers which had spoken to the young men of the time " with an emphasis that hindered them from sleep," is strikingly true of his own writings. His first slim, anonymous duodecimo, *Nature*, was as fair and fascinating to the royal young minds who met it in the course of their reading, as Egeria to Numa wandering in the grove. The essays, orations, and poems followed, developing and elaborating the same spiritual and heroic philosophy, applying it to life, history, and literature, with a vigor and richness so supreme, that not only do many account him our truest philosopher, but others acknowledge him as our most characteristic poet.

It would be a curious inquiry how

much and what kind of influence the placid scenery of Concord has exercised upon his mind. "I chide society, I embrace solitude" he says; "and yet I am not so ungrateful as not to see the wise, the lovely, and the noble minded, as from time to time they pass my gate." It is not difficult to understand his fondness for the spot. He has been always familiar with it, always more or less a resident of the village.

Born in Boston, upon the spot where the Chauncey Place Church now stands, part of his youth was passed in the Old Manse, which was built by his grandfather, and in which his father was born; and there he wrote *Nature*. From the magnificent admiration of ancestral England, he was glad to return to quiet Concord, and to acres which will not yield a single arrowhead.

The Swiss sigh for their mountains; but the Nubians pine for their desert plains. Those who are born by the sea long annually to return, and to rest their eyes upon its living horizon. Is it because the earliest impressions, made when the mind is most plastic, are most durable, or because youth is that golden age bounding the confines of memory, and floating forever an alluring mirage as we recede farther from it?

The imagination of the man who roams the solitary pastures of Concord, or floats dreamily down its river, will easily see its landscape upon Emerson's pages. "That country is fairest," he says, "which is inhabited by the noblest minds."

And although that idler upon the river may have leaned over the Mediterranean from Genoese and Neapolitan villas, or have glanced down the steep, green valley of Sicilian Enna, or walked the shores where Cleopatra and Helen walked, yet the charm of a landscape which is felt, rather than seen, will be imperishable. "Travelling is a Fool's Paradise," says Emerson. But he passed Concord's gates to learn that lesson. His writings, however, have no imported air. If there be something Oriental in his philosophy and tropical in his imagination, they have yet the strong flavor of his Mother Earth, the underived sweetness of the open Concord sky, and the spacious breadth of the Concord horizon.

BRYANT

43

His youth was innocent ; his riper age
  Marked with some act of goodness every day ;
And watched by eyes that loved him, calm and
    sage,
  Faded his late declining years away.
Meekly he gave his being up, and went
To share the holy rest that waits a life well spent.

The Old Man's Funeral.

FOREWORD

THERE is a tender tribute to the memory of Mrs. Kirkland, written by Mr. Bryant at the time of her death, in 1864. "A beautiful soul," wrote the Editor of *The Post* . . . "one whom I was proud to call my friend."

In the sketch presented here, friend writes of friend. Mr. Bryant had done much in bringing Mrs. Kirkland's books before the public, and it was meet that gratitude and affection should flow when she took up her pen to write of him. But Bryant's name deserves all the good and gracious things that Mrs. Kirkland says, and if Mr. Bryant's judgment was a bit blinded by friendship when he called Mrs. Kirkland's books "sublime" and "immortal," why, what boots it? Love is ever blind and friendship is quite near-sighted—and I am glad.

E. H.

BRYANT.

BY CAROLINE H. KIRKLAND.*

—

IF ever there were poet of whom it is not necessary to ask whether he lives in town or country, it is Mr. Bryant. Not even Burns gives more unmistakable signs of the inspiration of rural sights and sounds. Winds breathe soft or loud; sunshine or shadow flits over the landscape; leaves rustle and birds sing wherever his verses are read. The ceiling overhead becomes a forest with green boughs waving; the carpet turns to fresh grass, and the air we breathe is moist and fragrant with mosses and hidden streams.

* Written in 1853 for Putnam's *Homes of American Authors.*

No need of carrying the book out-of-doors
to aid the illusion ; its own magic is irresistible, and brings out-of-doors wherever
it goes.   Here is a mind whose

> Raptures are not conjured up
> To serve occasion of poetic pomp,
> But genuine—

and such as could not be excited or satis-
fied with pictures of what it loves.

It is consistent, therefore, when we find
the poet's home a great, old-time mansion, so embosomed in trees and vines that
we can hardly catch satisfactory glimpses
of the bay on which it lies, through the
leafy windows, of which an overhanging
roof prolongs the shade. No greener, qui-
eter, or more purely simple retreat can be
found ; none with which the owner and
his tastes and occupations are more in
keeping.   It would be absurd to say that
all appearance of show or style is carefully avoided for it requires very little
observation to perceive that these are
absent from the place simply because
they never entered its master's mind.

I suppose if anything could completely displease Mr. Bryant with this beloved home, it would be the addition of any outward costliness, or even elegance, calculated to attract the attention of the passing stranger. Friend Richard Kirk —a Quaker of the Quakers, if he may be judged by his works—little thought, when he built this great, ample, square dwelling-place, in the lap of the hills, in 1787, that he was fashioning the house of a poet—one worthy to be spared when temple and tower went to the ground, because it is the sanctuary of a priest of Nature.

Whether any captain, or colonel, or knight in arms did spare it, from a prophetic insight into its destination, we cannot tell ; but there was wild work in its vicinity, and stories of outrages perpetrated by " cow-boys " and other desperadoes are still fresh in old families. The wide region still called Hempstead was then inhabited for the most part by loyalists, devoutly attached to the parent

government, and solicitous, by means of
town meetings passing loyal resolutions,
and conventions denouncing the spirit
of rebellion against "his most gracious
majesty, King George the Third," to put
down the dangerous agitation that began
to threaten "our civil and religious liberties, which can only be secured by our
present constitution"; and this northern part of the township, in particular,
held many worthy citizens who felt it
their duty to resist to the last the unhal-
lowed desire of the people to govern
themselves.

In September, 1775, an official reports
that "without the assistance of Col. Lash-
er's battalion" he "shall not be able, in
Jamaica and Hempstead, to carry the
resolutions of Congress into execution,"
as "the people conceal all their arms
that are of any value." The disaffection
of the district was considered important
enough to justify a special commission
from Congress, then sitting at Philadelphia, requiring the resistants to deliver

their arms and ammunition on oath, as persons "incapable of resolving to live and die freemen, and more disposed to quit their liberties than part with the small portion of their property that may be necessary to defend them."

This seems to have had the desired effect, for the people not only brought in their arms, but were "much irritated with those who had led them to make opposition," says a contemporary letter. The lovers of peace and plenty, rather than commotion and scanty harvests, were, however, still so numerous in Queen's County, that on the 21st of October, 1776, about thirteen hundred freeholders presented a most humble petition to Lord Howe, entreating that he would "declare the County in the peace of His Majesty," and denouncing "the infatuated conduct of the Congress," as having "blasted their hopes of returning peace and security." Among the names appended to this petition we find that of Richard Kirk,—a lover of comfort, doubt-

less, like his brethren in general,—and
who, when once the drum had ceased to
outrage the mild echoes of that Quaker
region, returned to his farming or his
merchandise, and in due season, being
prospered, founded the substantial dwelling now known as Spring Bank, destined
to last far into the time of freedom and
safety, and to prove, in these latter days,
fit harbor for a poet whose sympathies
are anywhere but with the signers of that
humble petition.

The house stands at the foot of a woody
hill, which shelters it on the east, facing
Hemstead Harbor, to which the flood-tide
gives the appearance of a lake, bordered
to its very edge with trees, through which,
at intervals, are seen farm-houses and cottages, and all that brings to mind that
beautiful image, "a smiling land." The
position is well chosen, and it is enhanced
in beauty by a small artificial pond, collected from the springs with which the
hill abounds, and lying between the house
and the edge of the harbor, from which it

is divided by an irregular embankment, affording room for a plantation of shade-trees and fine shrubbery. Here again Friend Richard was doing what he little thought of; for his only intention was to build a paper-mill—one of the earliest in the United States, whose wheel for many a year furnished employment to the out-let of the pond. The mill was burnt once and again—by way of hint, perhaps, that beauty is use enough,—and the visitor cannot but hope it will never be rebuilt.

The village at the head of the harbor was long called North Hempstead, but as there were already quite Hempsteads enough in Queen's County to perplex future topographers, the inhabitants united in desiring a more distinctive title, and applied to Mr. Bryant for his aid in choosing one. This is not so easy a matter as it seems at first glance; and in defect of all express guidance in the history of the spot, and desiring, too, a name at once musical in itself and agree-able in its associations, Mr. Bryant proposed Roslyn,—the town annals declaring that when the British evacuated the island in 1781, "The Sixtieth, or Royal American Regiment, marched out of Hempstead to the tune of Roslyn Castle." The name is not too romantic for the place, for a more irregular, picturesque cluster of houses can hardly be found, perched here and there on the hillsides, embowered in foliage, and looking down upon a chain of pretty little lakes, on the outlet of which, overhanging the upper point of the harbor, is an old-fashioned mill with its pretty rural accessories. One can hardly believe this a bit of Long Island, which is by no means famed for romantic scenery.

After Richard Kirk's time, other Quakers in succession became proprietors of the great farm-house and the little paper-mill, but at length they were purchased by Joseph W. Moulton, Esq., author of a history of New York, who, not relishing the plainness of the original style, surrounded the house with square columns

and a heavy cornice. These help to shade
a wide and ample piazza, shut in still
more closely by tall trees and clustering
vines, so that from within, the house is
one bower of greenery, and the hottest
sun of July leaves the ample hall and
large rooms cool and comfortable.

The library occupies the northwest
corner—and we need hardly say that
of all the house this is the most attractive spot, not only because, besides ample
store of books, it is supplied with all that
can minister to quiet and refined pleasure, but because it is, par excellence,
the haunt of the poet and his friends.
Here, by the great table covered with
periodicals and literary novelties, with
the soft, ceaseless music of rustling leaves,
and the singing of birds making the silence sweeter, the summer visitor may
fancy himself in the very woods, only
with a deeper and more grateful shade.
And when wintry blasts are piping loud
and the whispering leaves have changed
to whirling ones, a bright wood-fire lights

the home scene, enhanced in comfort by
the inhospitable sky without; and the
domestic lamp calls about it a smiling or
musing circle, for whose conversation or
silence the shelves around afford excellent
material. The collection of books is not
large, but widely various; Mr. Bryant's
tastes and pursuits leading him through
the entire range of literature, from the
Fathers to Shelley, and from Courier to
Jean Paul. In German, French, and
Spanish he is proficient, and Italian he
reads with ease; so all these languages
are well represented in the library. He
turns naturally from the driest treatise on
politics or political economy to the wild-
est romance or the most tender poem,
happy in a power of enjoying all that
genius has created or industry achieved
in literature.

The library has not, however, power to
keep Mr. Bryant from the fields, in which
he seeks health and pleasure a large part
of every day that his editorial duties allow him to pass at home. To explore

his farm, entering into the minutest details of its cultivation; to thread the beautiful woodland hill back of the house, making winding paths and shady seats to overlook the water or command the distant prospect; to labor in the garden with the perseverance of an enthusiast—these ought, perhaps, to be called his favorite occupations; for as literature has been the business of his life, these out-door pleasures have all the charm of contrast together with that of relaxation.

And it is under the open sky, and engaged in rural matters, that Mr. Bryant is seen to advantage, that is, in his true character. It is here that the amenity and natural sweetness of disposition, sometimes clouded by the cares of life and the untoward circumstances of business intercourse, shine gently forth under the influences of Nature, so dear to the heart and tranquilizing to the spirits of her child. Here the eye puts on its deeper and softer lustre, and the voice modulates itself to the tone of affection, sympathy, and enjoyment. Little children cluster about the grave man's steps, or climb his shoulders in triumph ; and serenest eyes meet his in fullest confidence, finding there none of the sternness of which casual observers sometimes complain. It seems almost a pity that other walks should ever draw him hence ; but perhaps the contrast between garden walks and city pavements is required for the perfection and durability of rural pleasures.

There can hardly be found a man who has tried active life for fifty years, yet preserved so entire and resolute a simplicity of character and habits as Mr. Bryant. No one can be less a man of the world—so far as that term expresses a worldly man—in spite of a large share of worldly travel and extensive intercourse with society. A disposition somewhat exclusive, and a power of living self-inclosed at will, may account in part for the total failure of politics, society, or ambition to introduce anything artificial upon a character enabled by natural courage to

face opposition, and by inherent self-re-
spect to adhere to individual tastes in
spite of fashion or convention.

And the simplicity which is the result
of high cultivation is so much more potent than that which arises only from ig-
norance, that it may be doubted whether,
if Mr. Bryant had never left his native
village of Cummington, in the heart of
Massachusetts, he would have been as
free from all sophistication of taste and
manners as at present. It is with no
sentimental aim that I call him the child
of Nature, but because he is one of the
few who, by their docility and devotion,
show that they are not ashamed of the
great Mother or desirous to exchange her
rule for something more fashionable or
popular.

The father of Mr. Bryant was a man
of taste and learning—a physician and an
habitual student ; and his mother—not to
discredit the general law which gives able
mothers to eminent men—was a woman
of excellent understanding and high char-

acter, remarkable for judgment and decision as for faithfulness to her domestic
duties. And here, in this little village
of Cummington,—where William Cullen
Bryant was born in 1794,—he began at
ten years of age to write verses, which
were printed in the Northampton newspaper of that day—the *Hampshire Gazette.* A year earlier he had written
rhymes, which his father criticised and
taught him to correct.

Precocity like this too often disap-
points its admirers, but Bryant went on
without faltering, and at fourteen wrote
a satirical poem called the *Embargo*,
which is, perhaps, one of the most wonderful performances of the kind on record.
We know of nothing to compare with it
except the achievements of Chatterton.

Here are a few of the lines—would you
think a child penned them?

E'en while I sing, see Faction urge her claim,
Misled with falsehood, and with zeal inflame ;
Lift her black banner, spread her empire wide,
And stalk triumphant with a Fury's stride.
She blows her brazen trump, and, at the sound,

A motley throng, obedient, flock around ;
A mist of changing hue o'er all she flings,
And darkness perches on her dragon wings !
O, might some patriot rise ! the gloom dispel,
Chase Error's mist, and break her magic spell !
But vain the wish, for, hark ! the murmuring
     meed
Of hoarse applause from yonder shed proceed ;
Enter, and view the thronging concourse there,
Intent with gaping mouth and stupid stare ;
While, in the midst, their supple leader stands,
Harangues aloud, and flourishes his hands ;
To adulation tunes his servile throat,
And sues, successful, for each blockhead's vote.

This poem was published in company with a few shorter ones, at Boston, in 1808. A short time afterward the author entered Williams College, and greatly distinguished himself during two years, at the end of which time he obtained an honorable discharge, intending to complete his education at Yale—a design which was, however, never carried into effect. He studied law, first with Judge Howe of Washington, afterwards with Mr. William Baylies of Bridgewater, and in 1815 was admitted to the bar at Plymouth. He practised law a single year at Plainfield, near his native place, and then removed to Great Barrington, in Berkshire, where, in 1821, he married Miss Frances Fairchild, whose portrait is exquisitely shadowed forth, to those who know her, in that tenderest, most domestic, and most personal poem that Bryant ever wrote, *The Future Life*. In the whole range of English literature there can hardly be found so delicate and touching a tribute to feminine excellence —a husband's testimony after twenty years of married life, not exempt from toils and trials.

The poem of *Thanatopsis* was written in 1812, when the writer was eighteen. I once heard a family friend say that when Dr. Bryant showed a copy to a lady well qualified to judge of such things, saying simply: "Here are some lines that our William has been writing," the lady read the poem, raised her eyes to the father's face, and burst into tears, in which that father, a somewhat stern and silent man, was not ashamed to join. And no wonder! It must have seemed a mystery, as well as a joy, that in a quiet country life, in the heart of eighteen, had grown up thoughts that even in boyhood shaped themselves into solemn harmonies, majestic as the diapason of ocean, fit for a temple-service beneath the vault of heaven.

The poem of the *Water Fowl* was written two years after, while Mr. Bryant was reading law at Bridgewater. These verses, which are in tone only less solemn than *Thanatopsis*, while they show a graphic power truly remarkable, were suggested by the actual sight of a solitary water-fowl, steadily flying towards the northwest at sunset, in a brightly illumined sky. They were published, with *Thanatopsis* and the *Inscription for the Entrance to a Wood*, in the *North American Review* of the year 1816.

In 1821 Mr. Bryant delivered the poem called *The Ages* before the Phi Beta Kappa Society at Cambridge. At the suggestion of his friends it was published the same year, at Cambridge, together with the three poems just mentioned, and a very few others, among which was that called *Green River*, which he had a short time before contributed to the *Idle Man*, then in course of publication by his friend Dana.

In 1824 Mr. Bryant wrote a considerable number of papers for the *Literary Gazette*, published in Boston ; and in 1825, by the advice of his excellent and lamented friend, Henry D. Sedgwick, he removed to New York, and became one of the editors of the *New York Review*, in conjunction with Henry James Anderson. At the end of six months this gentleman, between whom and Mr. Bryant there has ever since subsisted a strong friendship, was appointed Professor of Mathematics in Columbia College, and Robert C. Sands took his place as associate editor of the *Review*. The *Review*, however, was not destined to as long a life as it deserved—the life of *Reviews* as well as of men depending upon a multitude of contingencies—and at the end of the year Mr. Bryant was engaged as an

HOME OF BRYANT, Roslyn, Long Island, N. Y.

assistant editor of the *Evening Post*. The
next year he became one of the proprietors of that paper, and has so continued
ever since.

In 1827, and the two years next suc-
ceeding, he found time to contribute a
considerable share of the matter of an
annual of superior character, called the
Talisman, the whole of which was written by three persons—Sands, Verplanck,
and Bryant. He also furnished several
stories for a publication called *Tales of
the Glauber Spa*, published by the Harpers. The other writers were Miss Sedgwick, Paulding, Sands, Verplanck, and
Leggett. Mr. Bryant's contributions were
The Skeleton's Cave and *Medfield*.

The first general collection of his works
was in 1832, when he gave to the world
in one volume all the poems he was willing to acknowledge. His publisher was
Mr. Elam Bliss, now no more, a man of
whose sterling goodness Mr. Bryant loves
to speak, as eminent for exemplary liberality in dealings, and for a most kind and

generous disposition. It was for him that the *Talisman* was written.

In 1834 Mr. Bryant sailed with his family to Europe, leaving the *Evening Post* in the charge of his friend Leggett. His residence abroad was mostly in Italy and Germany, both of which countries he found too interesting for a mere glance. Here the pleasure and improvement of himself and his family would have detained him full three years—the allotted period of his sojourn abroad—but news of Mr. Leggett's illness, and of some disadvantage arising from it in the affairs of the paper, compelled him to return home suddenly in 1836, leaving his family to follow at more leisure under the care of Mr. Longfellow, who had been abroad at the same time. The business aspect of the *Post* was unpromising enough at this juncture, but sound judgment and patient labor succeeded, in time, in restoring it to the prosperous condition which it has enjoyed for half a century.

In 1842 appeared *The Fountain*, gravely

sweet, like its predecessors, and breathing of Nature and green fields, in spite
of editorial and pecuniary cares. In 1843,
Mr. Bryant refreshed himself by a visit
to the Southern States, and passed a few
weeks in Florida. The *White-Footed
Deer*, with several other poems, was published a year after. In 1845, Mr. Bryant
visited England, Scotland, and the Shet-
land Isles for the first time ; and during
the next year a new collection was made
of his poems, with the outward garnish
of mechanical elegance, and also numerous illustrations by Leutze. This edition,
published at Philadelphia, is enriched
with a beautiful portrait by Cheney—the
best, in our opinion, ever yet published.
This graceful and delicate head, with its
fine, classic outline, in which taste and
sensitiveness are legible at a glance, has
a singular resemblance to the engraved
portraits of Rubens, taken in a half-Span-
ish hat of wavy outline, such as Mr. Bryant is fond of wearing in his wood-rambles.
Add the hat to this exquisite miniature

of Cheney's, and we have Rubens complete—an odd enough resemblance, when we contrast the productions of the painter and the poet.

Only one still more characteristic and perfect likeness of Bryant exists—the full-length in Durand's picture of the poet standing with his friend Cole—the eminent landscape-painter—among the Catskill woods and waterfalls. This picture is particularly to be prized, not only for the sweetness and truth of its general execution, but because it gives us the poet and the painter where they loved best to be, and just as they were when under the genial influence and in the complete ease of such scenes. Such pictures are half biographies.

In 1848 Cole died, and Mr. Bryant, from a full heart, pronounced his funeral oration. Friendship is truly the wine of the poet's life, and Cole was a beloved friend. If Mr. Bryant ever appears stern or indifferent, it is not when speaking or thinking of the loved and lost. No man chooses

his friends more carefully ; none prizes
them dearer, or values their society more
—none does them more generous and delicate justice. Such attachment cannot
afford to be indiscriminate.

March, 1849, saw Mr. Bryant in Cuba,
and in the summer of the same year he
visited Europe for the third time. The
letters written during his various journeys
and voyages were collected and published
in the year 1850 by Mr. George Palmer
Putnam. They comprise a volume em-
bodying a vast amount of practical and
poetic thought expressed with the united
modesty and good sense that so eminently
characterize every production of Mr.
Bryant ; not a superfluous word, not an
empty or a showy remark. As a writer
of pure, manly, straightforward English,
Mr. Bryant has few equals and no supe-
riors among us.

In the beginning of 1852, on the occasion of the public commemoration held
in honor of the genius and worth of James
Fenimore Cooper, and in view of a monu-

ment to be erected in New York to that great American novelist, Mr. Bryant pronounced a discourse on his life and writings, marked by the warmest appreciation of his claims to the remembrance and gratitude of his country. Some even of Mr. Cooper's admirers objected that the poet had assigned a higher niche to his old friend than the next century will be willing to award him ; if it be so, perhaps the peculiarly manly and bold character of Cooper's mind gave him an unsuspected advantage in Mr. Bryant's estimation. He looked upon him, it may be, as a rock of truth and courage in the midst of a fluctuating sea of dilletantism and time-serving, and valued him with unconscious reference to this particular quality, so rare and precious. But the discourse was an elegant production, and a new proof of the generosity with which Mr. Bryant, who never courts praise, is disposed to accord it.

Mr. Bryant's habits of life have a smack of asceticism, although he is the disciple of none of the popular schools which, under various forms, claim to rule the present world in that direction. Milk is more familiar to his lips than wine. He eats sparingly of animal food, but he is by no means afraid to enjoy roast goose lest he should outrage the names of his ancestors, like some modern enthusiasts. He loves music, and his ear is finely attuned to the varied harmonies of wood and wave. His health is delicate, yet he is very seldom ill ; his life laborious, yet carefully guarded against excessive and exhausting fatigue. He is a man of rule, but none the less tolerant of want of method in others ; strictly self-governed, but not prone to censure the unwary or the weak-willed. In religion he is at once catholic and devout, and to moral excellence no soul bows lower.

Placable we can perhaps hardly call him, for impressions on his mind are almost indelible ; but it may with the strictest truth be said, that it requires a great offence, or a great unworthiness, to make

an enemy of him, so strong is his sense
of justice. Not amid the bustle and dust
of the political arena, cased in armor offensive and defensive, is a champion's
more intimate self to be estimated, but
in the pavilion or the bower, where, in
robes of ease, and with all professional
ferocity laid aside, we see his natural
form and complexion, and hear in placid
and domestic tones the voice so lately
thundering above the fight.

So we willingly follow Mr. Bryant to
Roslyn; see him musing on the pretty
rural bridge that spans the fish-pond; or
taking the oar in his daughter's fairy
boat; or pruning his trees; or talking
over farming matters with his neighbors;
or—to return to the spot whence we set
out some time ago—sitting calm and
happy in that pleasant library, surrounded
by the friends he loves to draw about him,
or listening to the prattle of infant voices,
quite as much at home there as under
their own more especial roof—his daughter's—within the same enclosure.

In person Mr. Bryant is tall, slender, symmetrical, and well-poised; in carriage eminently firm and self-possessed. He is fond of long rural walks and of gymnastic exercises—on all which his health depends. Poetical composition tries him severely—so severely that his efforts of that kind are necessarily rare. His are no holiday verses; and those who urge his producing a long poem are, perhaps, proposing that he should, in gratifying their admiration, build for himself a monument with a crypt beneath.

Let us rather content ourselves with asking "a few more of the same," especially of the later poems, in which, certainly, the poet trusts his fellows with a nearer and more intimate view of his inner and peculiar self than was his wont in earlier times. Let him more and more give a human voice to woods and waters; and, in acting as the accepted interpreter of Nature, speak fearlessly to the heart as well as to the eye. His countrymen were never more disposed to hear him

with delight; for since the public de-
mand for his poems has placed a copy
in every house in the land, the taste for
them has steadily increased, and the national pride in the writer's genius become a generous enthusiasm, which is
ready to grant him an apothesis while he
lives.

PRESCOTT.

With the benevolent mission of Gasca then the historian of the *Conquest* may be permitted to terminate his labors,—with feelings not unlike those of the traveller, who, having long journeyed among the dreary forests and dangerous defiles of the mountains, at length emerges on some pleasant landscape smiling in tranquillity and peace.

Conquest of Peru.

FOREWORD

Mr. George S. Hillard, who wrote this essay in 1852, was a lawyer with a liking for letters. He was a personal friend of Mr. Prescott's, and such an admirer of the historian's work that when he published unsigned articles, people often said "Prescott"—and then was Mr. Hillard greatly pleased. His style is as broadly generous and calmly flowing as the Niagara just below the Falls: only a Lake Erie of words, and a cataract of ideas could supply it. And if he chose to speak of a man's mother as his "immediate maternal ancestor," or a boatride as "an aquatic excursion" it surely was his legal right.

E. H.

PRESCOTT

—

BY GEO. S. HILLARD.*

THE true idea of a home includes something more than a place to live in. It involves elements which are intangible and imponderable. It means a particular spot in which the mind is developed, the character trained, and the affections fed. It supposes a chain of association, by which mute material forms are linked to certain states of thoughts and moods of feeling, so that our joys and sorrows, our struggles and triumphs, are chronicled on the walls of a house, the trunk of a tree, or the walks of a garden.

* Written in 1853 for Putnam's *Homes of American Authors.*

Many persons are so unhappy as to pass through life without these sweet influences. Their lives are wandering and nomadic, and their temporary places of shelter are mere tents, though built of brick or wood. The bride is brought home to one house, the child is born in another, and dies in a third. As we walk through the unexpressive squares of one of our cities, and mark their dreary monotony of front, and their ever-changing door-plates, how few of these houses are there that present themselves to the eye with any of these symbols and indications of home. These, we say instinctively, are mere parallelograms of air, with sections and divisions at regular intervals, in which men may eat and sleep, but not live, in the large meaning of the term.

But a country-house, however small and plain, if it be only well placed, as in the shadow of a patriarchal tree, or on the banks of a stream, or in a hollow of a sheltering hill, has more of the look of home than many a costly city mansion.

In the former, a portion of nature seems to have been subdued and converted to the uses of man, and yet its primitive character to have remained unchanged ; but, in the latter, nature has been slain and buried, and a huge brick monument erected to her memory. We read that "God setteth the solitary in families." The significance of this beautiful expression dwells in its last word. The solitary are not set in hotels or boarding-houses, nor yet in communities or phalausteries, but in families. The burden of solitude is to be lightened by household affections, and not by mere aggregation. True society—that which the heart craves and the character needs—is only to be found at home, and what are called the cares of house-keeping, from which so many selfishly and indolently shrink, when lighted by mutual forbearance and unpretending self-sacrifice, become occasion of endearment and instruction of moral and spiritual growth.

The partial deprivation of sight under

which Mr. Prescott has long labored, is
now a fact in literary history almost as
well known as the blindness of Milton
or the lameness of Scott. Indeed,
many magnify in their thoughts the
extent of his loss, and picture to themselves the author of "Ferdinand and
Isabella" as a venerable personage,
entirely sightless, whose "dark steps"
require a constant "guiding hand," and
are greatly surprised when they see this
ideal image transformed into a figure re-
taining a more than common share of
youthful lightness of movement, and a
countenance full of freshness and anima-
tion, which betrays to a casual observation no mark of visual imperfection.
The weight of this trial, heavy indeed to
a man of literary tastes, has been balanced in Mr. Prescott's case by great
compensations. He has been happy in the
home he has made for himself, and happy
in the troops of loving and sympathizing
friends whom he has gathered around
him. He has been happy in the early

possession of that leisure which has enabled him to give his whole energies to literary labors, without distraction or interruption, and most of all, happy in his own genial temper, his cheerful spirit, his cordial frankness, and that disposition to look on the bright side of men and things, which is better not only than house and land, but than genius and fame. It is his privilege, by no means universal with successful authors, to be best valued where most known ; and the graceful tribute which his intimate friend, Mr. Ticknor, has paid to him, in the preface to his *History of Spanish Literature*, that his " honors will always be dearest to those who have best known the discouragements under which they have been won, and the modesty and gentleness with which they are worn," is but an expression of the common feeling of all those who know him.

To come down to smaller matters, Mr. Prescott has been fortunate in the merely local influences which have helped to

train his mind and character. His lines
have fallen to him in pleasant places.
His father, who removed from Salem to
Boston when he himself was quite young,
lived for many years in a house in Bedford
Street, now swept away by the march of
change, the effect of which, in a place of
limited extent like Boston, is to crowd
the population into constantly narrowing
spaces. It was one of a class of houses
of which but few specimens are now left
in our densely settled peninsula.

It was built of brick, painted yellow,
was square in form, and had rooms on
either side of the front door. It had little
architectural merit and no architectural
pretension. But it stood by itself, and
was not imprisoned in a block, had a few
feet of land between the front door and
the street, and a reasonable amount of
breathing-space and elbow-room at the
sides and in the rear, and was shaded by
some fine elms and horse-chestnuts. It
had a certain individual character and
expression of its own. Here Mr. Prescott

the elder, commonly known and addressed in Boston as Judge Prescott, lived from 1817 to 1844, the year of his death.

Mr. Prescott the younger, the historian, upon his marriage, did not leave his father's house to seek a new home, but, complying with a kindly custom more common in Europe, at least upon the Continent, than in America, continued to reside under the paternal roof, the two families forming one united and affectionate household, which, in the latter years of Judge Prescott's life, presented most engaging forms of age, mature life, and blooming youth. As Mr. Prescott's circle of research grew wider, the house was enlarged by the addition of a study, to accommodate his books and manuscripts, and here fame found him living when she came to seek him after the publication of the *History of Ferdinand and Isabella.* No one of those who were so fortunate as to enjoy the friendship of both the father and the son ever walks by the spot where this house once stood, without recalling with a mingling of pleasure and of pain its substantial and respectable appearance, its warm atmosphere of welcome and hospitality, and the dignified form, so expressive of wisdom and of worth, of that admirable person who so long presided over it. This house was pulled down a few years since, soon after the death of Judge Prescott; his son having previously removed to the house in Beacon Street, in which he now lives during the winter months.

Few authors have ever been so rich in dwelling-places as Mr. Prescott. "The truth is," says he in a letter to Mr. George P. Putnam, "I have three places of residence, among which I contrive to distribute my year. Six months I pass in town, where my house is in Beacon Street, looking on the Common, which, as you may recollect, is an uncommonly fine situation, commanding a noble view of land and water."

There is little in the external aspect of this house in Beacon Street to distinguish

it from others in its immediate vicinity.
It is one of a continuous but not uniform
block. It is of brick, painted white, four
stories high, and with one of those swelled
fronts which are characteristic of Boston.
It has the usual proportion and distribution of drawing-rooms, dining-room, and
chambers, which are furnished with unpretending elegance and adorned with
some portraits, copies of originals in
Spain, illustrative of Mr. Prescott's writings. The most striking portion of the
interior consists of an ample library,
added by Mr. Prescott to the rear of the
house, and communicating with the
drawing-rooms. It is an apartment of
noble size and fine proportions, filled with
a choice collection of books, mostly historical, which are disposed in cases of
richly-veined and highly-polished oak.
This room, which is much used in the
social arrangements of the household, is
not that in which Mr. Prescott does his
hard literary work. A much smaller
apartment, above the library and com-

municating with it, is the working study
—an arrangement similar to that adopted
by Sir Walter Scott at Abbotsford.

Mr. Prescott's collection of books has
been made with special reference to his
own departments of inquiry, and in these
it is very rich. It contains many works
which cannot be found in any other private library, at least, in this country.
Besides these, he has a large number of
manuscripts, amounting in the aggregate
to not less than twenty thousand folio
pages, illustrative of the periods of history treated in his works. These manuscripts have been drawn from all parts of
Europe, as well as from the States of
Spanish origin in this country. He has
also many curious and valuable auto-
graphs.

Nor is the interest of this apartment
confined to its books and manuscripts.
Over the window at the northern end,
there are two swords suspended, and
crossed like a pair of clasped hands.
One of these was borne by Colonel Pres-

cott at Bunker Hill, and the other by Captain Linzee, the maternal grandfather of Mrs. Prescott, who commanded the British sloop of war *Falcon*, which was engaged in firing upon the American troops on that occasion. It is a significant and suggestive sight, from which a thoughtful mind may draw out a long web of reflection. These swords, once waving in hostile hands, but now amicably lying side by side, symbolize not merely the union of families once opposed in deadly struggle, but, as we hope and trust, the mood of peace which is destined to guide the two great nations which, like parted streams, trace back their source to the same parent fountain.

On entering the library from the drawing-room, the visitor sees at first no egress except by the door through which he has just passed; but, on his attention being called to a particular space in the populous shelves, he is, if a reading man, attracted by some rows of portly quartos and goodly octavos, handsomely bound, bearing inviting names, unknown to Lowndes or Brunet. On reaching forth his hand to take one of them down, he finds that while they keep the word of promise to the eye, they break it to the hope, for the seeming books are nothing but strips of gilded leather pasted upon a flat surface, and stamped with titles, in the selection of which, Mr. Prescott has indulged that playful fancy which, though it can rarely appear in his grave historical works, is constantly animating his correspondence and conversation. It is, in short, a secret door, opening at the touch of a spring, and concealed from observation when shut. A small winding staircase leads to a room of moderate extent above, so arranged as to give all possible advantage of light to the imperfect eyes of the historian. Here Mr. Prescott gathers around him the books and manuscripts in use for the particular work on which he may be engaged, and few persons, except himself and his secretary, ever penetrate to this studious retreat.

In regard to situation, few houses in any city are superior to this. It stands directly upon the Common, a beautiful piece of ground, tastefully laid out, molded into an exhilerating variety of surface, and only open to the objection of being too much cut up by the intersecting paths which the time-saving habits of the thrifty Bostonians have traced across it. Mr. Prescott's house stands nearly opposite a small sheet of water, to which the tasteless name of Frog Pond is so inveterately fixed by long usage, that it can never be divorced from it. Of late years, since the introduction of the Cochituate water, a fountain has been made to play here, which throws up an obelisk of sparkling silver, springing from the bosom of the little lake, like a palm-tree from the sands, producing, in its simple beauty, a far finer effect than some of the costly architectural fancies of Europe.

Here a beautiful spectacle may be seen in the long afternoons of June, before the midsummer heats have browned the grass, when the crystal plumes of the fountain are waving in the breeze, and the rich, yellow light of the slow-sinking sun hangs in the air and throws long shadows on the turf, and the Common is sprinkled, far and wide, with well-dressed and well-mannered crowds—a spectacle in which not only the eye but the heart also may take pleasure, from the evidence which it furnishes of the general diffusion of material comfort, worth and intelligence. Here in the early days of spring, the timid crocus and snowdrop peep from the soil long before the iron hand of winter has been lifted from the rest of the city. Besides the near attraction of the Common, which is beautiful in all seasons, this part of Boston, from its elevated position, commands a fine view of the western horizon, including a range of graceful and thickly-peopled hills in Brookline and Roxbury. Our brilliant winter sunsets are seen here to the greatest advantage. The whole western sky burns with rich metallic lights of orange,

yellow, and yellow-green ; the outlines
of the hills in the clear, frosty air, are
sharply cut against this glowing back-
ground ; the wind-harps of the leafless
trees send forth a melancholy music, and
the faint stars steal out one by one as the
shrouding veil of daylight is slowly withdrawn. A walk at this hour along the
western side of the Common offers a
larger amount of the soothing and eleva-
ting influences of nature than most dwell-
ers in cities can command.

In this house in Beacon Street, Mr.
Prescott lives for about half the year, engaged in literary research, and finding re-
lief from his studies in the society of a
numerous circle of friends, a precious
possession, in which no man is more rich.
Few persons in our country are so exclu-
sively men of letters. His time and
energies are not at all given to the exciting and ephemeral claims of the passing
hour, but devoted to those calm researches
the results of which have appeared in his
published works. He is strongly social

in his tastes and habits, and his manners and conversation in society are uncommonly free from that stiffness and coldness which are apt to creep over students. He retains more of youthful ease and unreserve than most men, whatever be their way of life, carry into middle age. He is methodical in his habits of exercise as well as of study, and is much given to long walks, as in former years to long rides. These periods of exercise, however, are not wholly idle. From his defective sight he has acquired the habit (not a very common one) of thinking without the pen, and many a smooth period has been wrought and polished in the forge of the brain while in the saddle or on foot.

The occupants of most of the houses in that part of Boston where Mr. Prescott lives, are birds of passage. As soon as the sun of our short-lived summer puts off the countenance of a friend, and puts on that of a foe, one by one they take their flight. House after house shuts up

its green lids, and resigns itself to a three
or four months' sleep. The owners distribute themselves among various places
of retreat, rural, suburban or marine,
more or less remote. Mr. Prescott also
quits the noise, dust and heat of Boston
at this season, and takes refuge for some
weeks in a cottage at Nahant. "This
place," he writes to the publisher, "is a
cottage—what Lady Emeline Stuart Wort-
ley calles in her *Travels* 'a charming
country villa' at Nahant, where for more
than twenty years I have passed the summer months, as it is the coolest spot in
New England. The house stands on a
bald cliff, overlooking the ocean, so near
that in a storm the spray is thrown over
the piazza, and as it is located on the extreme point of the peninsula, is many
miles out at sea. There is more than one
printed account of Nahant, which is a remarkable watering-place, from the bold
formation of the coast and its exposure
to the ocean. It is not a bad place—this
sea-girt citadel—for reverie and writing,

with the music of the winds and waters incessantly beating on the rocks and broad beaches below. This place is called 'Fitful Head,' and Norna's was not wilder."

The peninsula of Nahant, which Mr. Prescott has thus briefly described, is a rocky promontoy, running out to sea from the mainland of Lynn, to which it is connected by a straight beach, some two or three miles in length, divided into two unequal portions by a bold headland called Little Nahant. It juts out abruptly, in an adventurous and defying way, and laid down on a map of a large scale, it looks like an outstretched arm with a clenched fist at the end of it. Thus going out to sea to battle with the waves on our stormy New England coast, it is built of the strongest materials which the laboratory of Nature can furnish. It is a solid mass of the hardest porphyritic rock, over which a thin drapery of soil is thrown. At the southern extremity this wall of rock is broken into grand, irregular forms, and seamed and scarred with

HOME OF PRESCOTT, Pepperell, Mass.

the marks of innumerable conflicts. A
lover of Nature in her sterner moods
can find few spots of more attraction
than this presents after a south-easterly
storm. The dark ridges of the rapid
waves leap upon the broken cliffs with an
expression so like that of animal rage,
that it is difficult to believe that they are
not conscious of what they are about. But
in an instant the gray mass is broken into
splinters of snowy spray, which glide and
hiss over the rocky points and hang their
dripping and fleecy locks along the sheer
wall, the dazzling white contrasting as
vividly with the reddish brown of the
rock, as does the passionate movement
with the monumental calm. One is never
weary of watching so glorious a spectacle,
for though the elements remain the same,
yet, from their combination, there results
a constant variety of form and movement.
Nature never repeats herself. As no two
pebbles on a beach are identical, so no
two waves ever break upon a rock in precisely the same way.

The beach which connects the headland of little Nahant with the mainland
of Lynn, is about a mile and a half long,
and curved into the finest line of beauty.
At low tide there is a space of some twenty
or thirty rods wide, left bare by the receding waters. This has a very gentle
inclination, and having been hammered
upon so long by the action of the waves,
it is as hard and smooth as a marble floor,
presenting an inviting field for exercise,
whether on foot, in carriages, or on horseback. The wheels roll over it in silence
and leave no indentation behind, and even
the hoofs of a galloping steed make but
a momentary impression. On a fine
breezy afternoon, in the season, when the
tide is favorable, this beach presents a
most exhilarating spectacle, for the whole
gay world of the place is attracted here :
some in carriages, some on horseback,
and some on foot. Every kind of carriage that American ingenuity has ever
devised is here represented, from the old-
fashioned family coach, with its air of

solid, church and state respectability, to
the sporting man's wagon, which looks
like a vehicular tarantula, all wheels and
no body. The inspiriting influence of
the scene extends itself to both bipeds
and quadrupeds. Little boys and girls
race about on the fascinating wet sand,
so that their nurses, what with the waves
and what with the horses' hoofs, are kept
in a perpetual frenzy of apprehension.
Sober pedestrians, taking their "consti-
tutional" involuntarily quicken their
pace, as if they were really walking for
pleasure in the coolness and moisture under them. Fair equestrians dash across
the beach at full gallop, their veils and
dresses streaming on the breeze, attended
by their own flying shadows in the smooth
watery mirror of the yellow sands. Let
the waves curl and break in long lines of
dazzling foam and spring upon the beach
as if they enjoyed their own restless
play; sprinkle the bay with snowy sails
for the setting sun to linger and play
upon, and cover the whole with a bright

blue sky dappled with drifting clouds,
and all these elements make up so animating a scene, that a man must be very
moody or very apathetic not to feel his
heart grow lighter as he gazes upon it.

The position of Nahant, and its convenient distance from Boston, makes it a
place of much resort in the hot months
of Summer. There are many hotels and
boarding-houses ; and also a large number of cottages, occupied for the most
part by families, the heads of which come
up to town every day and return in the
evening. The climate and scenery are so
marked, that they give rise to very decided opinions. Many pronounce Nahant
delightful, but some do not hesitate to
call it detestable. No place can be more
marine and less rural. There are no
woods and very few trees. There are
none but ocean sights and ocean sounds.
It is like being out at sea in a great ship
that does not rock. As every wind blows
off the bay, the temperature of the air is
very low, and the clear green water looks

cold enough in a hot August noon to
make one's teeth chatter, so that it requires some resolution to venture upon a
bath, and still more to repeat the experiment. The characteristic climate of Nahant may be observed in one of those
days not uncommon on the coast of New
England, when a sharp east wind sets in
after a hot morning. The sea turns up a
chill steel-blue surface, and the air is so
cold that it is not comfortable to sit still
in the shade, while the sky, the parched
grass, the dusty roads, and the sunshine
bright and cold, like moonbeams, give to
the eye a strangely deceptive promise of
heat. Under the calm light of a broad,
full moon, Nahant puts on a strange and
unearthly beauty. The sea sparkles in
silver gleams, and its phosphoric foam is
in vivid contrast with the inky shadows
of the cliffs. The ships dart away into
the luminous distance, like spectral forms.
In the deep stillness, the sullen plunge
of the long, breaking waves becomes op-
pressive to the spirits. The roofs of the

cottages glitter with spiritual light, and the white line of the dusty road is turned into a path of pearl.

The cottage which Mr. Prescott occupies at Nahant is built of wood, two stories in height and has a spacious piazza running round it, which in fine weather is much used as a supplementary drawing-room. There is nothing remarkable whatever in its external appearance. Its plain and unassuming aspect provokes neither criticism nor admiration. Its situation is one of the finest in the whole peninsula. It stands upon the extremity of a bold, bluff-like promontory, and its elevated position gives it the command of a very wide horizon. The sea makes up a large proportion of the prospect, and as every vessel that sails into or out of the harbor of Boston passes within range of the eye, there is never a moment in which the view is not animated by ships and canvas. The pier, where the steamer which plies between Boston and Nahant, lands and receives her passengers, and the Swallow's Cave, one of the sights of the place, are both within a stone's-throw of the cottage.

Mr. Prescott resides at Nahant from eight to ten weeks, and finds a refreshing and restorative influence in its keenly bracing sea-air. This, though a season of retirement, is by no means one of indolence, for he works as many hours every day and accomplishes as much, here, as in Boston, his time of study being comparatively free from those interruptions which in a busy city will so often break into a scholar's seclusion. As his life at Nahant falls within the travelling season, he receives here many of the strangers who are attracted to his presence by his literary reputation and the report of his amiable manners. And this tribute to celebrity, exacted in the form of golden hours from every distinguished man in our enterprising and inquisitive age, is paid with a cheerful good-humor, which leaves no alloy in the recollections of those who have thus enjoyed the privilege of his society.

Mr. Prescott's second remove—for if poor Richard's saying be strictly true, he is burnt out every year—is from Nahant to Pepperell, and usually happens early in September. His home in Pepperell is thus described by him in a letter to Mr. Putnam :

"The place at Pepperell has been in the family for more than a century and a half, an uncommon event among our locomotive people. The house is about a century old, the original building having been greatly enlarged by my father first, and since by me. It is here that my grandfather, Col. Wm. Prescott, who commanded at Bunker Hill, was born and died, and in the village church-yard he lies buried under a simple slab, containing only the record of his name and age. My father, Wm. Prescott, the best and wisest of his name, was also born and passed his earlier days here, and, from my own infancy, not a year has passed that

I have not spent more or less of in these shades, now hallowed to me by the recollection of happy hours and friends that are gone.

"The place, which is called 'The Highlands,' consists of some two hundred and fifty acres, about forty-two miles from Boston, on the border-line of Massachusetts and New Hampshire. It is a fine, rolling country; and the house stands on a rising ground that descends with a gentle sweep to the Nissitisset, a clear and very pretty little river, affording picturesque views in its winding course. A bold mountain chain on the northwest, among which is the Grand Monadnoc, in New Hampshire, makes a dark frame to the picture. The land is well studded with trees—oak, walnut, chestnut, and maple—distributed in clumps and avenues, so as to produce an excellent effect. The maple, in particular, in its autumn season, when the family are there, makes a brave show with its gay livery when touched by the frost."

To possess an estate like that at Pepperell, which has come down by lineal
descent through several successions of
owners, all of whom were useful and
honorable men in their day and generation, is a privilege not common any
where, and very rare in a country like
ours, young in years and not fruitful in
local attachments. Family pride may be
a weakness, but family reverence is a
just and generous sentiment. No man
can look round upon fields of his own
like those at Pepperell, where, to a suggestive eye, the very forms of the landscape seem to have caught an expression
from the patriotism, the public spirit, the
integrity, and the intelligence which now
for more than a hundred years have been
associated with them, without being conscious of a rush of emotions, all of which
set in the direction of honor and virtue.

The name of Prescott has now, for
more than two hundred years, been
known and honored in Massachusetts.
The first of the name, of whom mention

is made, was John Prescott, who came to this country in 1640, and settled in Lancaster. He was a blacksmith and millwright by trade—a man of athletic frame and dauntless resolution; and his strength and courage were more than once put to the proof in those encounters which so often took place between the Indians and the early settlers of New England. He brought with him from England a helmet and suit of armor—perhaps an heirloom descended from some ancestor who had fought at Poitiers, or Flodden-field—and whenever the Indians attacked his house he clothed himself in full mail and sallied out against them; and the advantages he is reported to have gained were probably quite as much owing to the terror inspired by his appearance as to the prowess of his arm.

His grandson, Benjamin Prescott, who lived in Groton, was a man of influence and consideration in the colony of Massachusetts. He represented Groton for many years in the colonial legislature, was a magistrate, and an officer in the militia. In 1735 he was chosen agent of the province to maintain their rights in a controversy with New Hampshire respecting boundary lines, but declined the trust on account of not having had the small-pox, which was prevalent at the time in London. Mr. Edmund Quincy, who was appointed in his place, took the disease and died of it. But, in the same year, the messenger of fate found Mr. Prescott upon his own farm, engaged in the peaceful labors of agriculture. He died in August, 1735, of a sudden inflammatory attack, brought on by over-exertion, in a hot day, to save a crop of grain from an impending shower. He was but forty years old at the time of his death, and the influence he had long enjoyed among a community slow to give their confidence to the young, is an expressive tribute to his character and understanding. He had the further advantage of a dignified and commanding personal appearance. In 1735, the year of his death, he received a donation of about eight hundred acres of land from the town of Groton for his servies in procuring a large territory for them from the General Court, and the present family estate in Pepperell forms probably a part of this grant.

His second son was Col. Wm. Prescott, the commander of the American forces at the Battle of Bunker Hill, who, after his father's death, and while he was yet in his minority, settled upon the estate in Pepperell, and built the house which is still standing. Up to the age of forty-nine, his life, with the exception of a few months' service in the old French war, was passed in agricultural labors, and the discharge of those modest civic trusts which the influence of his family, and the confidence inspired by his own character, devolved upon him. Joining the army at Cambridge immediately after the news of the Concord fight, it was his good fortune to secure a permanent place in history, by commanding the troops of his country in a battle, to which subsequent events gave a significance greatly disproportioned both to the numbers engaged in it and to its immediate results. At the end of the campaign of 1776, he returned home and resumed his usual course of life, which continued uninterrupted, except that he was present as a volunteer with General Gates at the surrender of Burgoyne, until his death, 1795, when he was in his seventieth year. He was a man of vigorous mind, not much indebted to the advantages of education in early life, though he preserved to the last a taste for reading. His judgment and good sense were much esteemed by the community in which he lived, and were always at their service both in public and private affairs. He was of a generous temper, and somewhat impaired his estate by his liberal spirit and hearty hospitality. In the career of Colonel Prescott we see how well the training given by the institutions of New England fits a man for discharging worthily the

duties of war or peace. We see a man
summoned from the plough, and by the
accident of war called upon to perform
an important military service, and in the
exercise of his duty we find him display-
ing that calm courage and sagacious
judgment which a life in the camp is
supposed to be necessary to bestow. Nor
was his a rare case, for as the needs
of our revolutionary struggle required
such men, they were always forthcoming.
Nor is there any reason to suppose that
Colonel Prescott, himself, ever looked
upon his conduct on the seventeenth of
June as anything to be especially com-
mended, but only as the performance of a
simple piece of duty, which could not have
been put by without shame and disgrace.

Judge Prescott, who died in Boston in
the month of December, 1844, at the age
of eighty-two, was the only child of Colonel Prescott, and born upon the family
estate at Pepperell. His son, in one of
his quoted letters, speaks of him as "the
best and wisest of his name." It does

not become a stranger to their blood to
confirm or deny a comparative estimate
like this, but all who knew Judge Prescott will agree that he must have gone
very far who would have found a wiser
or a better man. His active life was
mainly passed in the unambitious labors
of the bar; a profession which often
secures to its members a fair share of substantial returns and much local influence,
but rarely gives extended or posthumous
fame. He had no taste for political life,
and the few public trusts which he discharged was rather from a sense of duty
than from inclination.

The town of Pepperell lies in the northern part of the county of Middlesex,
bordering upon the State of New Hampshire. Its inhabitants are mostly farmers,
cultivating their own lands with their own
hands—a class of men which forms the
best wealth of a country, the value of
whom we never properly estimate till
we have been in regions where they have
ceased to exist. The soil is of that rea-

souable and moderate fertility, common in New England, which gives constant motive to intelligent labor, and rewards it with fair returns—a kind of soil very favorable to the growth of the plant, man. The character of the scenery is pleasing, without any claim to be called striking or picturesque. The land rises and falls in a manner that contents the eye, and the distant horizon is dignified by some of those high hills to which, in our magniloquent way, we give the name of mountains. The town has the advantage of being watered by two streams, the Nashua and the Nissitisset. The former is a thrifty New England river that turns mills, furnishes water-power, and works for its living in a respectable way; the latter is a giddy little stream that does little else than look pretty; gliding through quiet meadows fringed with alder and willow, tripping and singing over pebbly shallows, and expanding into tranquil pools, gemmed with white water-lilies, the purest and most spiritual of flowers.

Mr. Prescott's farm is about two miles
from the centre of the town, in a region
which has more than the average amount
of that quiet beauty characteristic of New
England scenery. The house stands upon
rather high ground, and commands an
extensive view of a gently-undulating
region, most of which is grass land, which
when clothed in the " glad, light green "
of our early summer, and animated with
flying cloud-shadows, presents a fine and
exhilerating prospect. As the farm has
been so long under cultivation, and as
for many years past the claims of taste
and the harvests of the eye have not been
overlooked in its management, the landscape in the immediate neighborhood of
the house has a riper and a mellower look
than is usual in the rural parts of New
England. At a short distance in front,
on the opposite side of the road, sloping
gently down to the meadows of the Nissitisset, is a smooth symmetrical knoll, on
which are some happily-disposed clumps
of trees, so that the whole has the air of

a scene in an English park. The meadows and fields beyond are also well supplied with trees, and the morning and evening shadows which fall from these, as well as from the rounded heights, give character and expression to the landscape.

The house itself has little to distinguish it from the better class of New England farm-houses. It wears our common uniform of white, with green blinds; is long in proportion to its height, and the older portions bear marks of age. There is a piazza, occupying one side and a part of the front. Since it was first built there have been several additions made to it—some recently, by Mr. Prescott himself—so that the interior is rambling, irregular and old-fashioned, but thoroughly comfortable, and hospitably arranged, so as to accommodate a large number of guests. These are sometimes more numerous than the family itself. There is a small fruit and kitchen garden on the east side of the house, and on the west, as also in front, is a grassy lawn, over which many young feet have sported and frolicked, and some that were not young.

The great charm of the house consists in the number of fine trees by which it is surrounded and overshadowed. These are chiefly elms, oaks, maples and butternuts. Of these last there are some remarkably large specimens. From these trees the house derives an air of dignity and grace which is the more conspicuous from the fact that these noble ornaments to a habitation are not so common in New England as is to be desired. Our agricultural population have not yet shaken off those transmitted impressions derived from a period when a tree was regarded as an enemy to be overcome. Would that the farmers of fifty years ago had been mindful of the injunction given by the dying Scotch laird to his son, " Be aye sticking in a tree, Jock ; it will be growing while you are sleeping." What a different aspect the face of the country might have been made to wear. A bald and staring farm-house, shivering in the winter wind, or fainting in the summer sun, without a rag of a tree to cover its nakedness with, is a forlorn and unsightly object, rather a blot upon the landscape than an embellishment to it.

Behind the house, which faces the south, the ground rises into a considerble elevation, upon which there are also several fine trees. A small oval pond is nearly surrounded by a company of graceful elms, which, with their slender branches and pensile foliage, suggest to a fanciful eye a group of wood-nymphs smoothing their locks in the mirror of a fountain. At a short distance, a clump of oaks and chestnuts, which look as if they had been sown by the hand of art, have formed a kind of natural arbor, the shade of which is inviting to meditative feet. Under these trees Mr. Prescott has passed many studious hours, and his steps, as he has paced to and fro, have worn a perceptible path in the turf. A few rods from the house, towards the east, is another and larger pond, near which is a

grove of vigorous oaks ; and, in the same
direction, about half a mile farther, is an
extensive piece of natural woodland,
through which winding paths are traced,
in which a lover of nature may soon bury
himself in primeval shades, under broad-
armed trees which have witnessed the
stealthy steps of the Indian hunter, and
shutting out the sights and sounds of
artificial life, hear only the rustling of
leaves, the tap of a wood-pecker, the
dropping of nuts, the whir of a partridge,
or the call of a sentinel crow.

The house is not occupied by the family during the heats of summer ; but they
remove to it as soon as the cool mornings
and evenings proclaim that summer is
over. The region is one which appears
to peculiar advantage under an autumnal
sky. The slopes and uplands are gay
with the orange and crimson of the maples, the sober scarlet and brown of the
oaks, and the warm yellow of the hicko-
ries. A delicate gold-dust vapor hangs in
the air, wraps the valleys in dreamy folds,

and softens all the distant outlines. The
bracing air and elastic turf invite to long
walks or rides ; the warm noons are delightful for driving ; and the country in
the neighborhood, veined with roads and
lanes that wind and turn and make no
haste to come to an end, is well suited for
all these forms of exercise. There is a
boat on the Nissitisset for those who are
fond of aquatic excursions, and a closet
full of books for a rainy day. Among
these are two works which seem in perfect unison with the older portion of the
house and its ancient furniture—Theo-
bald's *Shakespeare* and an **early** edition
of the *Spectator*—both bound in snuff-
colored calf, and printed on paper yellow
with age ; and the latter adorned with
those delicious copperplate engravings
which perpetuate a costume so ludicrously
absurd, that the wonder is that the wear-
ers could ever have left off laughing at
each other long enough to attend to any
of the business of life. When the cool
evenings begin to set in with something

of a wintry chill in the air, wood-fires are kindled in the spacious chimneys, which animate the low ceilings with their restless gleams, and when they have burned down, the dying embers diffuse a ruddy glow, which is just the light to tell a ghost-story by, such as may befit the narrow rambling passages of the old farmhouse, and send a rosy cheek to bed a little paler than usual.

While Mr. Prescott is at Pepperell, a portion of every day is given to study; and the remainder is spent in long walks or drives, in listening to reading, or in the social circle of his family and guests. Under his roof there is always houseroom and heart-room for his own friends and those of his children. Indeed, he has followed the advice of some wise man —Dr. Johnson, perhaps, upon whom all vagrant scraps of wisdom are fathered— and kept his friendships in repair, making the friends of his children his own friends. There are many persons, not members of the family, who have become extremely attached to the place, from the happy hours they have spent there. There may be seen upon the window-sill of one of the rooms a few lines in pencil, by a young lady whose beauty and sweetness make her a great favorite among her friends, expressing her sense of a delightful visit made there, some two or three years since. Had similar records been left by all, of the happy days passed under this roof, the walls of the house would be hardly enough to hold them.

And this sketch may be fitly concluded with the expression of an earnest wish that thus it may long be. May the future be like the past. May the hours which pass over a house honored by so much worth and endeared by so much kindness, bring with them no other sorrows than such us the providence of God has inseparably linked to our mortal state —such as soften and elevate the heart, and, by gently weaning it from earth, help to dress the soul for its new home.

JAMES RUSSELL LOWELL

To Charles F. Briggs.

ELMWOOD, *Aug*, 21, 1845.

My sorrows are not literary ones, but those
of daily life. I pass through the world and meet
with scarcely a response to the affectionateness
of my nature. Brought up in a very reserved
and conventional family, I cannot in society appear what I really am. I go out sometimes with
my heart so full of yearning towards my fellows
that the indifferent look with which even entire
strangers pass me brings tears into my eyes.
And then to be looked upon by those who *do*
know me (externally) as "Lowell the poet" it
makes me sick. Why not as Lowell the man—
the boy rather,—as Jemmy Lowell?

JAMES R. LOWELL.

How it strikes a contemporary is always interesting ; and inadvertence, like irrelevance, has its charm.   These things being true, this essay written forty-three years ago is valuable.   The author tells with a poorly masked boast that the grandfather of Mr. Lowell was a Member of Congress.   For the grandson no such leap into greatness was prophesied —it was too much !   And as for the Court of St. James, Mr. Briggs had n't imagination enough to dream of it.   Yet I remember when the papers announced that our plain Harvard professor had been appointed Minister to England we boys thought of the big shaggy dog that tagged him through the street, of the briar-wood pipe, and the dusty suit of gray, and we were struck dumb with amazement.

Then, when Mr. Briggs quotes *The Courtin'*, and gives his idea of "true poetry" and "art," we bethink us that we have a few ideas in this line ourselves, and pass on.

The reference to Maria White brings to mind *The Letters*, and we remember the poet's various references to this splendid woman.

Mr. Briggs admits that his subject is an abolitionist—'t were vain to deny it—but he is not an unreasonable fanatical abolitionist, for, mark you, even Southerners read his poetry. Well, I guess so! And, thus Mr. Briggs saves Mr. Lowell's reputation and his own—forsooth, for wise men trim ship; and a list to starboard is as bad as a list to port if you are an all 'round literary man with manuscript to market. So we think no more of Lowell on account of the Briggs' apology and no less of Briggs. A shifty loyalty is ever entertaining when viewed across the intervening years. And we smile, but the smile turns to a sigh when we remember that Briggs, like his fears, is now dust; and that in Mt. Auburn where three weeping willows stand guard, sleeps a beloved nephew of Lowell given to the cause that "raised such a commotion." A step away are simple little slate slabs that mark the graves of "James Russell Lowell, and Maria White, his wife."

JAMES RUSSELL LOWELL.

BY CHAS. F. BRIGGS.*

CAMBRIDGE is one of the very few towns in New England that is worth visiting for the sake of its old houses. It has its full share of turreted and bedomed cottages, of pie-crust battlements, and Athenian temples; but its chief glory, besides its elms, and "muses' factories," are the fine old wooden mansions, which seem to be indigenous to the soil on which they stand, like the stately trees that surround them. These well-preserved relics of our ante-revolutionary splendor are not calculated

* Written in 1853 for Putnam's *Homes of American Authors.*

127

to make us feel proud of our advance-
ment in architectural taste, since we
achieved our independence ; and we cannot help thinking that men who are fond
of building make-believe baronial castles,
never could have had the spirit to dream
of asserting their independence of the
old world.   People who are afraid to trust
their own invention in so simple a thing
as house-building, could never have
trusted themselves in the more important business of government-making. Yet
some of these fine old houses, that have
so manly and independent a look, were
built by stanch, conservative tories, who
feared republicanism, and had no faith at
all in the possibility of a state without a
king.

The stately old mansion in which the
poet Lowell was born, one of the finest
in the neighborhood of Boston, was built
by Thomas Oliver, the last royal Lieutenant-Governor of the province of Massachusetts, who remained true to his
allegiance, and after the Declaration of

Independence removed to England, where he died. In Eliot's Biographical Dictionary of the first settlers in New England, is the following brief account of this sturdy royalist :

" Thomas Oliver was the last Lieutenant-Governor under the crown. He was a man of letters, and possessed of much good nature and good breeding; he was affable, courteous, a complete gentleman in his manners, and the delight of his acquaintance. He graduated at Harvard College in 1753. He built an elegant mansion in Cambridge, and enjoyed a plentiful fortune. When he left America it was with extreme regret. He lived in the shades of retirement while in Europe, and very lately (1809) his death was announced in the public papers."

The character of the man might easily have been told from examining his house ; it bears the marks of a generous and amiable nature, as unerringly as such qualities are denoted by the shape of the head. Mean men do not build themselves such habitations. Much good nature is plainly traceable in its fine large rooms, and its capacious chimneys, which might well be called

The wind-pipe of good hospitalite.

It has a broad staircase with easy landings, and a hall wide enough for a traditionary duel to have been fought in it, when, like many of the neighboring mansions, it was occupied by revolutionary soldiers. Washington, too, was once entertained under its roof, and after the war it became the property of Elbridge Gerry, one of the signers of the Declaration of Independence, who lived in it, while he was Vice-President of the United States. At his death it was purchased from the widow of Gerry by its present owner, the Rev. Charles Lowell, father of the Poet, by whom it was beautified and improved. Dr. Lowell planted the greater part of the noble trees which now surround it, conspicuous among them being the superb elms from which it derives its name. The grounds of Elmwood are about thirteen acres in extent, and adjoin on one side the cemetery of Mount Auburn, where two of the Poet's children, Blanche and Rose, are buried. It was on the grave of his firstborn that the beautiful poem, full of heartfelt tenderness, called *The First Snow-fall*, was written.

Some of Lowell's finest poems have trees for their themes, and he appears to entertain a strong affection for the leafy patriarchs beneath whose branches he had played in his boyhood. In one of the many poems which have overflowed from his prodigal genius into the columns of obscure monthly and weekly periodicals, and have not yet been published in a volume, is one called *A Day in June*, in which occurs an exquisitely touching apostrophe to the "tall elm" that forms so conspicuous an object in the view of Elmwood drawn by our artist:

Snap, chord of manhood's tenser strain ;
To-day I will be a boy again ;
The mind's pursuing element,
Like a bow slackened and unbent,

In some dark corner shall be leant ;
The robin sings, as of old, from the limb,
The cat-bird crows in the lilac bush ;
Through the dim arbor, himself more dim,
Silently hops the hermit-thrush,
The withered leaves keep dumb for him ;
The irreverent buccaneering bee
Hath stormed and rifled the nunnery
Of the lily, and scattered the sacred floor
With haste-dropt gold from shrine to door :
There, as of yore,
The rich milk-tinging buttercup,
Its tiny polished urn holds up,
Filled with ripe summer to the edge,
The sun in his own wine to pledge ;
And one tall elm, this hundredth year
Doge of our leafy Venice here,
Who with an annual ring doth wed
The blue Adriatic overhead,
Shadows with his palatial mass
The deep canals of flowing grass,
Where grow the dandelions sparse
For shadows of Italian stars.

Lowell has studied in the life-school of poetry, and all the pictures which he has woven into the texture of his verse have been drawn directly from nature, His descriptions of scenery are full of local coloring, and, in his *Indian Summer Reverie*, there are so many accurate and vivid pictures of Elmwood and its neighborhood, of the "silver Charles,"

the meadows, the trees, the distant hills,
the colleges, "the glimmering farms,"
and "Coptic tombs," that we need hardly
do more than transfer them to our pages
to give a vivid picture of his home and
its associations.

There gleams my native village, dear to me,
Though higher change's waves each day are
    seen,
Whelming fields famed in boyhood's history,
Sanding with houses the diminished green ;
There, in the red brick, which softening time
    defies,
Stand square and stiff the Muses' factories ;
How with my life knit up in every well-known
    scene !

Beyond that hillock's house-bespotted swell,
Where Gothic chapels house the horse and chaise,
Where quiet cits in Grecian temples dwell,
Where Coptic tombs resound with prayer and
    praise
Where dust and mud the equal year divide,
There gentle Alston lived, and wrought and died,
Transfiguring street and shop with his illumined
    gaze.

In this brilliant descriptive poem he
exhibits his native town in a series of
changing pictures that bring the scenes
perfectly before us under all the varying

phases of the year. What landscape painter has given us such pictures as these of the approaches of a New England winter?

Or come when sunset gives its freshened zest,
Lean o'er the bridge and let the ruddy thrill,
  While the shorn sun swells down the hazy
      west,
Glow opposite ;—the marshes drink their fill
  And swoon with purple veins, then slowly fade
  Through pink to brown, as eastward moves the
      shade
Lengthening with stealthy creep, of Simond's
      darkening hill.

Later, and yet ere winter wholly shuts,
Ere through the first dry snow the runner grates,
  And the loath cart-wheel screams in slippery
      ruts.
While firmer ice the boy eager awaits,
  Trying each buckle and strap beside the fire,
  And until bed-time plays with his desire,
Twenty times putting on and off his new-bought
      skates.

Our poet was born at Elmwood on the 22d of February, 1819—the youngling of the flock, received his early education in Cambridge, and in 1838 graduated at Harvard, where his father and grandfather had graduated before him. After his "colleging" he studied law, and was admitted to the bar; but he had opened an office in Boston, to lure clients, a very little while, when he discovered that he and the legal profession were not designed for each other. There could not have been a more uncongenial and unprofitable pursuit than that of the law for a nature so frank and generous as that of Lowell's; and, happily for him, necessity, which knows no law, did not compel him, as it has many others, to stick to the law, for a living, against his inclinations. So he abandoned all thoughts of the ermine, and of figuring in sheepskin volumes, if he had ever indulged in any such fancies, which is hardly probable, and, turning his back on a profession which is fitly typified by a woman with a bandage over her eyes, he turned to his books and trees at Elmwood, determined on making literature his reliance for fame and fortune.

His first start in literature, as a business, ended disastrously. In company with his friend Robert Carter, he established a monthly magazine called the *Pioneer*, which, owing to the failure of his publishers, did not last longer than the third number ; but it was admirably well conducted, and made a decided impression on the literary public by the elevated tone of its criticisms, and the superiority of its essays to the ordinary class of magazine literature. Soon after the failure of the *Pioneer* he was married to Miss Maria White, of Watertown, a lady of congenial tastes, and as remarkable for her womanly graces and accomplishments, as for her elevated intellectual qualities. *The Morning Glory*, published in the last edition of his poems, was written by her. They have resided at Elmwood since their marriage, with the exception of a year and a half spent in Italy.

The ancestors of Lowell were among the earliest and most eminent settlers of New England, and there are but few Americans who could boast of a more honorable or distinguished descent. He was named after his father's maternal

HOME OF LOWELL, Cambridge, Mass.

grandfather, Judge James Russell, of Charlestown, an eminent person in the colony of Massachusetts, one of whose descendants, Lechmere Russell, a general in the British army, recently died at his seat of Ashford Hall in Shropshire. The founder of the Lowell family in Massachusetts was Percival Lowell, who settled in the town of Newbury in the year 1639. The Hon. John Lowell, the Poet's grandfather, was one of the most eminent lawyers in Massachusetts ; he was a representative in Congress, and being a member of the convention which framed the first constitution of his native State, he introduced the provision into the Bill of Rights which abolished slavery in Massachusetts.

The father of Mr. Lowell is a distinguished Congregational clergyman, who has been pastor of the West Church of Boston nearly fifty years, and is the author of several works of a religious character ; he graduated at Harvard, and was an intimate friend and class-mate of

Washington Alston.   He afterwards went
to Edinburgh, where he studied divinity,
and matriculated at the University there
at the same time with Sir David Brewster,
who was also a divinity student.

A few years ago, when Dr. Lowell was
in Scotland with his wife and daughter,
he paid a visit to Melrose Abbey, and
while there heard a man tell another that
Sir David Brewster would be with him
directly. He had not met the eminent
philosopher since they were students together, and did not know that he was in
the neighborhood of his old friend's
house, which he learned, on inquiry, was
the fact. When the philosopher appeared,
Dr. Lowell made himself known, and
found, from the heartiness of the embrace
he received, that an interval of forty
years had not diminished the attachment
of his early friend and companion.

The mother of the Poet was a native of
New Hampshire, and a sister of the late
Captain Robert T. Spence, of the U. S.
Navy. She was a woman of remarkable

mind, and possessed in an eminent degree the power of acquiring languages, a faculty which is inherited by her daughter, Mrs. Putnam, whose controversy with Mr. Bowen, editor of the *North American Review*, respecting the late war in Hungary, brought her name so prominently before the public that there can be no impropriety in alluding to her here. Mrs. Putnam is probably one of the most remarkable of linguists, and there have been but few scholars whose philological learning has been greater than hers. She converses readily in French, Italian, German, Polish, Swedish, and Hungarian, and is familiar with twenty modern dialects, besides Greek, Latin, Hebrew, Persic, and Arabic. Mrs. Putnam made the first translation into English of Frederica Bremer's novel of *The Neighbors*, from the Swedish. The translation by Mary Howitt was made from the German.

The maternal ancestors of Lowell were of Danish origin, and emigrated to Amer-

ica from Kirkwall, in the Orkneys.
While Dr. Lowell was in Scotland with
his family, they went to the Orkneys to
visit the burial-place of his wife's fore-
fathers, and while there they met a cousin,
a native of England, whom Mrs. Lowell
had never before seen, who had been
many years in India, and on his return
to his native land, had gone, like her, on
a pious pilgrimage to visit the graves of
his ancestors.

Among all the authors whose homes
are noticed in this series, Lowell is the
only one who has the fortune to reside
in the house in which he was born. It
is a happiness which few Americans of
mature age can know. But Lowell has
been peculiarly happy in his domestic
relations ; Nature has endowed him with
a vigorous constitution and a healthy and
happy temperament ; and, but for the
loss of his three children, the youngest
of whom, his only boy, died recently in
Rome, there would have been fewer shadows on his path than have fallen to the

lot of most other poets. A nature like
his can make its own sunshine, and find
an oasis in every desert ; yet it was a
rare fortune that he found himself in such
a home as his imagination would have
created for him, if he had been cast
homeless upon the world. He loves to
throw a purple light over the familiar
scene, and to invest it with a superflu-
ousness of grateful gilding. The large-
hearted love to give, whether their gifts
be needed or not. The lovely landscape
around Elmwood looks still lovelier in
his verse than to the unaided vision ; and
the "dear marshes" through which the
briny Charles ebbs and flows, are pleas-
anter for being seen through the golden
haze of the Poet's affection :

Below, the Charles—a stripe of nether sky,
Now hid by rounded apple-trees between,
  Whose gaps the misplaced sail sweeps bellying
    by,
Now flickering golden through a woodland
    screen,
  Then spreading out, at his next turn beyond,
  A silver casket, like an inland pond –
Slips seaward silently through marshes purple
    and green.

Dear marshes ! vain to him the gift of sight
Who cannot in their various incomes share,
  From every season drawn, of shade and light,
Who sees in them but levels brown and bare ;
  Each change of storm or sunshine scatters free
  On them its largess of variety,
For nature with cheap means still works her
    wonders rare.

Elmwood is half a mile or so beyond the colleges, and lies off from the main street; the approach to it is through a pleasant green lane, or at least it was green when we last saw it, the trees having been freshly washed of their "brown dust" by a shower which was still falling, and the muddy division of the year having apparently just commenced. The house is so surrounded with trees that you catch but a glimpse of it until you stand opposite to it. Though built of wood, and nearly a century old, it shows no signs of decay. It is most appropriately furnished, and contains many interesting relics, old family pictures, and some choice works of art, among which are two busts by Powers, and two or three portraits by Page, among the finest he

has painted. Perhaps it may be gratifying to the reader to know that the Poet's
study, in which nearly all of his poems
have been written, is on the third floor,
in that far corner of the house on which,
in the engraving, the light falls so pleasantly.

Lowell is generally looked upon as a
serious poet, and, indeed, no one has a
better claim to be so regarded, for seriousness is one of the first essentials of all
genuine poetry. But seriousness is not
necessarily sadness. Much of his poetry
overflows with mirthful and jocund feelings, and, in his most pungent satire
there is a constant bubbling up of a genial
and loving nature; the brilliant flashes
of his wit are softened by an evident
gentleness of motive. He is the first of
our poets who has succeeded in making
our harsh and uncouth Yankee dialect
subservient to the uses of poetry; this he
has done with entire success in that admirable piece of humorous satire, *The
Bigelow Papers*. No productions of a

similar character, in this country, were
ever held so popular as the pithy verses of
Hosea Bigelow, in spite of their being so
strongly imbued with a trenchant spirit of
opposition to the popular political views
of the multitude ; and many of them have
been widely circulated by the newspapers
without any intimation being given of
their origin. We were sitting one evening in the bar-room of a hotel in Washington, just after the election of General
Taylor, when our poetical metropolis was
filled with office-seekers from all parts
of the country. The room was crowded
with rude men who were discussing
political matters, and the last thing we
could have looked for was a harangue
on American poetry. A roughly-dressed
down-easter, or at least he had the accent
and look of one, came into the bar-room,
and addressing himself to a knot of men
who appeared to know him, exclaimed,
"Who says there are no American
poets?" And he looked around upon
the company, as though he would be

rather pleased than otherwise to encounter an antagonist.

But nobody seemed disposed to venture such an assertion; the novelty of the question, however, attracted the attention of the people near him, which was probably all he wanted. "Well," continued the speaker, with an air of defiant confidence, "if anybody says so, I am prepared to dispute him. I have found an American poet. I don't know who he is, nor where he lives, but he is the author of these lines, and he is a poet." He took a newspaper from his pocket, and read what Parson Wilbur, in the *Bigelow Papers*, called a *New England Pastoral;*

> Zekle crep' up quite unbeknown,
>   An' peeked in thru the winder,
> An' there sot Huldy all alone,
>   'ith no one nigh to hender.

> Agin' the chimbly croonecks hung,
>   An' in amongst 'em rusted
> The ole queen's arm that gran'ther Young
>   Fetched back from Concord busted.

> The wannut logs shot sparkless out
>   Toward the pootiest, bless her!

An' leetle fires danced all about
  The chiny on the dresser.

The very room, coz she was in,
  Looked warm frum floor to ceilin',
An' she looked full as rosy agin
  Ez th' apples she wus peelin'.

She heerd a foot an' knowed it, tu,
  Araspin' on the scraper,—
All ways to once her feelins flew
  Like sparks in burnt-up paper.

He kin' o' l'itered on the mat,
  Some doubtfle o' the seekle ;
His heart kep' goin' pitypat,
  But hern went pity Zekle.

The Yankee read it with proper emphasis and an unctuous twang, and all the company agreed with him, that it was genuine poetry "and no mistake."

And so poetry makes its way in the crowd. If it have the true spirit in it, it will find a sure response in the great heart of the multitude, who are, after all, the only judges in art. There is no appeal from their decisions. And, in the case of Lowell, the decision was unmistakably in his favor. He is acknowledged as one of the poets of the people. There are none of our poets whose short pieces we find more frequently in the corners of newspapers, although they are but rarely attributed to their author.

Lowell's prose writings are as remarkable as his poetry ; the copiousness of his illustrations, the richness of his imagery, the easy flow of his sentences, the keenness of his wit, and the force and clearness of his reasoning, give to his reviews and essays a fascinating charm that would place him in the front rank of our prose writers, if he did occupy a similar position among our poets. He has written considerably for the *North American Review*, and some other periodicals, but the only volume of prose which he published, besides the *Bigelow Papers*, was the *Conversations on the Old Dramatists*, which appeared in 1849.

Lowell is naturally a politician, but we do not imagine he will ever be elected a member of Congress, as his grandfather was. He is such a politician as Milton was, and will never narrow himself down

to any other party than one which includes all mankind within its lines.   But
he cannot shut his eyes to the great movements of the day, and dally with his Muse,
when he can invoke her aid in the cause
of the oppressed and suffering.   He has
to contend with the disadvantages of a
reputation for abolitionism, which is as
unfavorable to the prospects of a poet as
of a politician ; but his abolitionism is of
a very different type from that which has
made so great a commotion among us
during the last ten or fifteen years.   Notwithstanding the unpopular imputation
which rests upon his name, it does not
appear to have made him enemies in the
South.   Some of his warmest and most
attached friends are residents of slave
States and are slave-holders ; and one of
the heartiest and most appreciative criticisms on his writings that have appeared
in this country was published in a Southern journal, a paper which can hardly be
suspected of giving aid and encouragement to any enemy of the South.

SIMMS

149

Lithe and long as the serpent train,
　　Springing and clinging from tree to tree,
Now darting upward, now down again,
　　With a twist and a twirl that are strange to see ;
Never took serpent a deadlier hold,
　　Never the cougar a wilder spring,
Strangling the oak with the boa's fold,
　　Spanning the beech with the condor's wing.

Yet no foe that we fear to seek,—
　　The boy leaps wild to thy rude embrace ;
Thy bulging arms bear as soft a cheek
　　As ever on lover's breast found place ;
On thy waving train is a playful hold
　　Thou shalt never to lighter grasp persuade ;
While a maiden sits in thy drooping fold,
　　And swings and sings in the noonday shade !

—The Grape-Vine Swing.

150

FOREWORD

THIS sketch, from the pen of Mr. Bryant, was done "by request." Very possibly it was written and disposed of at a single sitting. It is straightforward, explicit, and to the point, like one of his *Evening Post* editorials. It is manly in sentiment, grammatically expressed, contains no dangerous logic, and can safely be recommended for the Young Person.

Bryant was born in 1794, and at the time of this writing was fifty-eight years old. Simms was twelve years his junior, but his name was among the very first of the writers of his time ; while Bryant was known only as an editor who had written some good verse and some not so good. In fact Bryant was a disappointment to his friends (as most gifted men are), for in *Thanatopsis* he set a pace that he never afterward equalled. And it was Greeley who said that he never ceased to regret the fact that Bryant did not die at twenty, for then the world could have

151

marvelled at the things he left unwrit
and shown the *Thanatopsis* as a sample
of the tomes that might have been.

But we of to-day are thankful for the
example of that well-rounded life with
its beautiful old age, frosty but kindly;
and I never take down a volume of the
Library of Poetry and Song without saying grace.

We may search in vain in America for
a school-boy of twelve who does not know
Bryant, but when I asked a gentlemanly
and intelligent attendant at the Boston
Public Library to fetch me any volume
of prose by Simms, he brought me *Sims
on Gynecology*. I gazed at the book with
lack-lustre eye, and shot just one re-
proachful glance at the attendant. And
it was then that that charming little old
gentleman in the dusty grey suit came
to me and divining my wants (as he always does), told me that no one to speak
of reads Simms now. Then he led me
back through a labyrinth of cases, and
amid a maze of shelves showed me rows
on rows of books labelled Simms that no
one ever calls for. "And I remember
the time when he was as popular as Mr.
Howells is to-day!" said the old gentleman.

As Nature works incessantly to cover the leaves of last year, so does Fate seek to hide the fame that yesterday loomed large. And although Mr. John Burroughs says, "Serene I fold my hands and wait," yet for the moment let us lay aside sentiment and admit that Chance plays a most important part in keeping alive the names of greatness gone. We live in a costermonger time, when virtue is not its own reward, when innocence is not a sufficient shield, and when merit, unpuffed, is soon forgot. It is not moth and rust, nor the incomparable excellence of the contemporaneous, that causes the old to be brushed into the dust-bin, but it is the poppy fumes of forgetfulness.

But in the interests of Truth let us admit that what we call the God of Chance is only another name for Law not Understood. It is so easy to dispose of the matter by the canting phrase i' the nose, "Merit is sure to win," but before it is fact it must be amended thus: "Merit is sure to win if well advertised." Good books, like good thread, good soap, good horse-shoe nails, and good baking powder, must be properly presented. Truth can stand alone, but no book is truth;

it is only an endeavor to express truth, and will die the death if not advertised by its enemies or its loving friends.

Six men in New England have made a lasting-place for themselves in American Letters. Their work was good, but this alone (with a single exception) would not have floated it. It was necessary that they should stand by each other, and they did. There was an unwritten agreement that Boston and Cambridge should protect their own. This was done through the cult of a great University, through the Lyceum, and through the magazines controlled by publishers that were party to the alliance. An occasional growl in the way of a *Fable for Critics*, only advertised all hands. And now from time to time elegant reprints of the works of these six men are gotten out by New York and Boston publishers, and magazines, societies, clubs, and descendants keep the work fresh before the people.

The books of J. G. Holland, Margaret Fuller, Geo. S. Hillard, Chas. F. Briggs, Henry T. Tuckerman, and others have sunk by their own weight, while the graceful and superficial writings of Willis may be said to have drifted into oblivion because of their lack of weight. The

work was good, but not good enough,
yet six of the old guard live, and I am
glad that this is so. And all the point I
would now make is that when Mr. Simms
moved from Massachusetts to South
Carolina he courted Oblivion and—won
her.

But genius is constantly being "discovered." See what Fitzgerald did for
Omar Khayyam, whose *Rubaiyat* is now
published in America by seventeen firms;
behold how Boyesen discovered Ibsen
and Howells sweeping the horizon with
his telescope on the lookout for a genius,
spied Tolstoy and cried "There she
blows!" remember how Thoreau introduced Ruskin to America and Emerson
brought out Carlyle. And so I await
the advent of some Columbus on the Sea
of Letters who shall give us back that
lost Atalantis, William Gilmore Simms,
who Mr. Bryant says wrote fifty volumes
—poems, plays, novels, histories, and
biographies. Some of these fifty books
may be crude and gushing, but others
there be that show a splendid insight
into truth, a delicate sensibility, a broad
and generous sympathy, and withal the
great and tender heart of a noble man.

E. H.

SIMMS.

BY WILLIAM CULLEN BRYANT.[*]

THE country residence of William Gilmore Simms is on the plantation of his father-in-law, Mr. Roach, in Barnwell District, South Carolina, near Midway, a railway station at just half the distance between Charleston and Augusta. Here he passes half the year, the most agreeable half in that climate,—its pleasant winter, and portions of its spring and autumn—in a thinly settled country divided into large plantations, principally yielding cotton, with smaller fields of maize, sweet pota-

* Written in 1853 for Putnam's *Homes of American Authors.*

toes, pea-nuts, and other productions of the region, to which sugar-cane has lately been added.

Forests of oak, and of the majestic long-leaved pine, surround the dwelling, interspersed with broad openings, and stretch far away on all sides. In the edge of one of these are the habitations of the negroes by whom the plantation is cultivated, who are indulgently treated and lead an easy life. The bridle-roads through these noble forests, over the hard white sand, from which rise the lofty stems of the pines, are very beautiful. Sometimes they wind by the borders of swamps, green in mid-winter with the holly, the red bay, and other trees that wear their leaves throughout the year, among which the yellow jessamine twines itself and forms dense arbors, perfuming the air in March to a great distance with the delicate odor of its blossoms. In the midst of these swamps rises the tall Virginia cypress, with its roots in the dark water, the summer haunt of the alligator, who sleeps away the winter in holes made under the bank. Mr. Simms, both in his poetry and prose, has made large and striking use of the imagery supplied by the peculiar scenery of this region.

The house is a spacious country dwelling, without any pretensions to architectural elegance, comfortable for the climate, though built without that attention to what a South Carolinian would call the unwholesome exclusion of the outer air which is thought necessary in these colder latitudes. Around it are scattered a number of smaller buildings of brick, and a little further stand rows and clumps of evergreens—the water-oak, with its glistening light-colored foliage, the live-oak, with darker leaves, and the Carolina bird-cherry, one of the most beautiful trees of the South, blooming before the winter is past, and murmuring with multitudes of bees. In one of the lower rooms of this dwelling, in the midst of a well-chosen library, many of the books which comprise the numerous catalogue of Mr. Simms' works were written.

Mr. Simms was born April 17, 1806, in the State of South Carolina. It was at first intended that he should study medicine, but his inclinations having led him to the law, he devoted himself to the study of that profession. His literary habits are very uniform. His working hours usually commence in the morning, and last till two or three in the afternoon, after which he indulges in out-door recreations, in reading, or society. If friends or visitors break into his hours of morning labor, which he does not often permit, he usually redeems the lost time at night, after the guests have retired. He is a late sitter, and consequently a late riser. Landscape gardening is one of his favorite pastimes, and the grounds adjoining his residence afford agreeable evidence of his good taste.

Mr. Simms is a man of athletic make.

HOME OF SIMMS, Woodlands, South Carolina.

A full muscular development, and a fresh complexion, give token of vigorous health, which however is not without its interruptions ; for although not indisposed to physical exertion, the inclination to mental activity in the form of literary occupation, predominates with him over every other taste and pursuit.

His manners, like the expression of his countenance, are singularly frank and ingenuous, his temper generous and sincere, his domestic affections strong, his friendships faithful and lasting, and his life blameless. No man ever wore his character more in the general sight of men than he, or had ever less occasion to do otherwise. The activity of mind of which I have spoken, is as apparent in his conversation as in his writings. He is fond of discussion, likes to pursue an argument to its final retreat, and is not unwilling to complete disquisition which others, in their ordinary discourse, would leave in outline. He has travelled extensively, mingling freely with all classes,

and has accumulated an apparently ex-
haustless fund of anecdotes and incidents,
illustrative of life and manners. These
he relates, with great zest and inimitable
humor, reproducing to perfection the peculiar dialect and tones of the various
characters introduced, whether sand-lap-
per, backwoodsman, half-breed, or negro.

His literary character has this peculiarity which I may call remarkable, that
writing as he does with very great rapidity, and paying little regard to the objec-
tions brought by others against what he
writes, he has gone on improving upon
himself. His first attempts in poetry
were crude and jejune. As he proceeded,
he left them immeasurably behind, in
command of materials and power of execution, till in his beautiful poem of *Atalantis*, the finest, I think, he has written,
his faculties seem to have nearly reached
their maturity in this department. One
of his pieces, entitled *The Edge of the
Swamp*, may be quoted here not only as
a specimen of his descriptive verse, but

as an illustration of the peculiar source
from which his imagery is derived :

'T is a wild spot and hath a gloomy look ;
The bird sings never merrily in the trees,
And the young leaves seem blighted. A rank
　　growth
Spreads poisonously round, with power to taint
With blistering dews the thoughtless hand that
　　dares
To penetrate the covert. Cypresses
Crowd on the dank, wet earth ; and, stretched at
　　length,
The cayman—a fit dweller in such home—
Slumbers, half buried in the sedgy grass,
Beside the green ooze where he shelters him,
A whooping crane erects his skeleton form,
And shrieks in flight. Two summer ducks
　　aronsed
To apprehension, as they hear his cry,
Dash up from the lagoon, with marvellous haste,
Following his guidance. Meetly taught by these,
And startled at our rapid, near approach,
The steel-jawed monster, from his grassy bed,
Crawls slowly to his slimy, green abode,
Which straight receives him. You behold him
　　now,
His ridgy back uprising as he speeds,
In silence, to the centre of the stream,
Whence his head peers alone. A butterfly

That, travelling all the day, has counted climes
Only by flowers, to rest himself awhile,
Lights on the monster's brow. The surly mute
Straightway goes down, so suddenly, that he,
The dandy of the summer flowers and woods,
Dips his light wings, and spoils his golden coat,
With the rank water of that turbid pond.
Wondering and vexed, the plumed citizen
Flies with an hurried effort, to the shore,
Seeking his kindred flowers:—but seeks in
     vain—
Nothing of genial growth may there be seen,
Nothing of beautiful ! Wild, ragged trees,
That look like felon spectres, fetid shrubs,
That taint the gloomy atmosphere—dusk shades,
That gather, half a cloud, and half a fiend
In aspect, lurking on the swamp's wild edge—
Gloom with their sternness and forbidding
     frowns
The general prospect. The sad butterfly,
Waving his lackered wings, darts quickly on,
And, by his free flight, counsels us to speed
For better lodgings, and a scene more sweet
Than these drear borders offer us to-night.

Mr. Simms' prose writings show a similar process of gradual improvement,
though in them the change is less
marked, owing to his having appeared

before the public as a novelist at a riper period of his literary life.   In all that he has written his excellences are unborrowed ; their merits are the development of original native germs, without any apparent aid from models.   His thoughts, his diction, his arrangement are his own : he reminds you of no other author ; even in the lesser graces of literary execution, he combines languages after no pattern set by other authors, however beautiful.

His novels have a wide circulation, and are admired for the rapidity and fervor of the narrative, their picturesque descriptions, the energy with which they express the stronger emotions, and the force with which they portray local manners.   His critical writings, which have appeared in the Southern periodicals and are quite numerous, are less known. They often, no doubt, have in them those imperfections which belong to rapid composition, but I must be allowed to single out from among them one example of great excellence, his analysis and estimate of the literary character of Cooper, a critical essay of great depth and discrimination, to which I am not sure that anything hitherto written on the same subject is fully equal. He published his *Lyrics*, in 1825, eighteen years ago; his longest and best poem, *Atalantis, a Story of the Sea*, in 1832; *Martin Faber, Guy Rivers, Yemasee, Partisan, Mellichampe*, and many others, in succession. The entire series of his works, poetry and prose, comprises about fifty volumes.

WHITMAN.

All seems beautiful to me.
I can repeat over to men and women, You have
    done such good to me I would do the same
    to you,
I will recruit for myself and you as I go.
I will scatter myself among men and women as
    I go,
I will toss a new gladness and roughness among
    them.

—Song of the Open Road

WHITMAN.

BY ELBERT HUBBARD.

I.

MAX NORDAU wrote a book—wrote it with his tongue in his cheek, a dash of vitriol in the ink, and with a pen that scratched.

And the first critic who seemed to place a just estimate on the work was Mr. Zangwill (who has no Christian name). Mr. Zangwill made an attempt to swear out a *writ de lunatico inquirendo* against his Jewish brother, on the ground that the first symptom of insanity is often the delusion that others are insane; and this being so, Dr. Nordau was not a safe subject to be at large. But the Assize of Public Opinion denied the petition and the dear people bought the book at from three to five dollars per copy. Printed in several languages, its sales have mounted to a hundred thousand volumes, and the author's net profit is full forty thousand dollars. No wonder is it that, with pockets full to bursting, Dr. Nordau goes out behind the house and laughs uproariously whenever he thinks of how he has worked the world !

If Dr. Talmage is the Barnum of Theology, surely we may call Dr. Nordau the Barnum of Science. His agility in manipulating facts is equal to Hermann's now-you-see-it and now-you-don't with pocket handkerchiefs. Yet Hermann's exhibition is worth the admittance fee and Nordau's book (seemingly written in collaboration with Jules Verne and Mark Twain) would be cheap for a dollar. But what I object to is Prof. Hermann's disciples posing as Sure-Enough Materializing Mediums and Prof. Lombroso's followers calling themselves Scientists, when each goes forth without scrip or purse with no other purpose than to supply themselves with both.

Yet it was Barnum himself who said that the public delights in being humbugged, and strange it is that we will not allow ourselves to be thimble-rigged without paying for the privilege.

Nordau's success hinged on his audacious assumption that the public knew nothing of the Law of Antithesis. Yet Plato explained that the opposite of things look alike, and sometimes *are* alike, and that was quite awhile ago.

The multitude answered : "Thou hast a devil " ; Many of them said : "He hath a devil and is mad" ; Festus said with a loud voice : " Paul, thou art beside thyself." And Nordau shouts in a voice more heady than that of Pilate, more throaty than that of Festus—"Mad—Whitman was—mad beyond the cavil of a doubt!"

In 1862, Lincoln, looking out of a window (before lilacs last in the dooryard bloomed) on one of the streets of Washington, saw a workingman in shirt sleeves go by. Turning to a friend, the President said: "There goes a *man!*" The exclamation sounds singularly like that of Napoleon on meeting Goethe. But the Corsican's remark was intended for the poet's ear, while Lincoln did not know who his man was, although he came to know him afterward.

Lincoln in his early days was a workingman—an athlete, and he never quite got the idea out of his head (and I am glad) that he was still a hewer of wood. He once told George William Curtis that he more than half expected yet to go back to the farm and earn his daily bread by the work that his hands found to do ; he dreamed of it nights, and whenever he saw a splendid toiler, he felt like hailing the man as brother and striking hands with him. When Lincoln saw Whitman strolling majestically past, he took him for a stevedore or possibly the foreman of a construction gang.

Whitman was fifty-one years old then. His long flowing beard was snow white and the shock that covered his Jove-like head was iron grey. His form was that of an Apollo who had arrived at years of discretion. He weighed even two hundred pounds and was just six feet high. His plain check cotton shirt was open at the throat to the breast; and he had an independence, a self-sufficiency, and withal a cleanliness, a sweetness, a gentleness, that told that, although he had a giant's strength, he did not use it like a giant. Whitman used no tobacco, neither did he apply hot and rebellious liquors to his blood and with unblushing forehead woo the means of debility and disease. Up to his fifty-third year he had never known a sick day, although at thirty his hair had begun to whiten. He had the look of age in his youth and the look of youth in his age that often marks the exceptional man.

But at fifty-three his splendid health was crowded to the breaking strain.

How? Through caring for wounded, sick, and dying men : hour after hour, day after day, through the long silent watches of the night. From 1864 to the day of his death in 1892, physically, he was a man in ruins. But he did not wither at the top. Through it all he held the healthy optimism of boyhood, carrying with him the perfume of the morning and the lavish heart of youth.

Doctor Bucke, who was superintendent of a hospital for the insane for fifteen years, and the intimate friend of Whitman all the time, has said : "His build, his stature, his exceptional health of mind and body, the size and form of his features, his cleanliness of mind and body, the grace of his movements and gestures, the grandeur, and especially the magnetism of his presence; the charm of his voice, his genial kindly humor; the simplicity of his habits and tastes, his freedom from convention, the largeness and beauty of his manner; his calmness and majesty; his charity and forbearance—his entire unresentfulness under whatever provocation ; his liberality, his universal sympathy with humanity in all ages and lands, his broad tolerance, his catholic friendliness, and his unexampled faculty of attracting affection, all prove his perfectly proportioned manliness."

But Whitman differed from the disciple of Lombroso in two notable particulars : He had no quarrel with the world, and he did not wax rich. " One thing thou lackest, O Walt Whitman!" we might have said to the poet, " you are not a financier." He died poor. But this is not proof of degeneracy save on 'Change. When the children of Count Tolstoy endeavored to have him adjudged insane, the Court denied the application and voiced the wisest decision that ever came out of Russia: A man who gives away his money is not necessarily more foolish than he who saves it.

And with Mr. Horace L. Traubel I say : Whitman was the sanest man I ever saw.

II

SOME men make themselves homes; and others there be who rent rooms. Walt Whitman was essentially a citizen of the world: the world was his home and mankind were his friends. There was a quality in the man peculiarly universal: a strong, virile poise that asked for nothing, but took what it needed.

He loved men as brothers, yet his brothers after the flesh understood him not; he loved children—they turned to him instinctively—but he had no children of his own; he loved women and yet this strongly sexed and manly man never loved a woman. And I might here say as Philip Gilbert Hamerton said of Turner, "He was lamentably unfortunate in this: throughout his whole life he never came under the ennobling and refining influence of a good woman."

It requires two to make a home. The first home was made when a woman, cradling in her loving arms a baby, crooned a lullaby. All the tender sentimentality we throw around a place is the result of the sacred thought that we live there with someone else. It is *our* home. The home is a tryst—the place where we retire and shut the world out. Lovers make a home just as birds make a nest, and unless a man knows the spell of the divine passion I hardly see how he can have a home at all. He only rents a room.

Camden is separated from the city of Philadelphia by the Delaware River. Camden lies low and flat—a great sandy, monotonous waste of straggling buildings. Here and there are straight rows of cheap houses, evidently erected by staid, broad-brimmed speculators from across the river, with eyes on the main chance. But they reckoned ill, for the town did not boom. Some of these houses have marble steps and white barn door shutters, that might withstand a siege. When a funeral takes place in one of these houses the shutters are tied with strips of mournful black alpaca for a year and a day. Engineers, dockmen, express drivers, and mechanics largely make up citizens of Camden. Of course, Camden has its smug corner where prosperous merchants most do congregate: where they play croquet in the front yards, and have window boxes, and a piano and veranda chairs and terra cotta statuary, but for the most part the houses of Camden are rented, and rented cheap.

Many of the domiciles are frame and have the happy tumble-down look of the back streets in Charleston or Richmond —those streets where white trash merges off into prosperous colored aristocracy. Old hats do duty in keeping out the fresh air where providence has interfered and broken out a pane; blinds hang by a single hinge; bricks on the chimney tops threaten the passers-by ; stringers and posts mark the place where proud picket fences once stood—the pickets having gone for kindling long ago. In the warm summer evenings men in shirt-sleeves sit on the front steps and stolidly smoke, while children pile up sand in the streets and play in the gutters.

Parallel with Mickle Street, a block away, are railway tracks. There noisy switch engines, that never keep Sabbath, puff back and forth, day and night, sending showers of soot and smoke when the wind is right (and it usually is) straight over Number 328, where, according to John Addington Symonds and William Michael Rossetti, lived the mightiest seer of the century—the man whom they rank with Socrates, Epictetus, St. Paul, Michael Angelo, and Dante.

It was in August of 1883 that I first walked up that little street—a hot sultry summer evening. There had been a shower that turned the dust of the unpaved roadway to mud. The air was close and muggy. The houses, built right up to the side-walks, over which in little gutters the steaming sewage ran, seemed to have discharged their occupants into the street to enjoy the cool of the day. Barefooted children by the score paddled in the mud. All the steps were filled with loungers; some of the men had discarded not only coats but shirts as well and now sat in flaming red underwear, holding babies.

They say that "woman's work is never done," but to the women of Mickle Street this does not apply, but stay! perhaps their work *is* never done. Anyway, I remember that women sat on the curbs in calico dresses or leaned out of the windows, and all seemed supremely free from care.

"Can you tell me where Mr. Whitman lives?" I asked a portly dame who was resting her elbows on a window-sill.

"Who?"

"Mr. Whitman!"

"You mean Walt Whitman?"

"Yes."

"Show the gentleman, Molly, he'll give you a nickel, I 'm sure!"

I had not seen Molly. She stood behind me, but as her mother spoke she seized tight hold of one of my fingers, claiming me as her lawful prey, and all the other children looked on with envious eyes as little Molly threw at them glances of scorn and marched me off. Molly was five, going on six, she told me. She had bright red hair, a grimy face and little chapped feet that made not a sound as we walked. She got her nickel and carried it in her mouth and this made conversation difficult. After going one block she suddenly stopped, squared me around and pointing said, "Them is he!" and disappeared.

In a wheeled rattan chair, in the hallway, a little back from the door of a plain weather-beaten house, sat the coatless philosopher, his face and head wreathed in a tumult of snow white hair.

I had a little speech, all prepared

weeks before and committed to memory, that I intended to repeat, telling him how I had read his poems and admired them. And further I had stored away in my mind a few blades from *Leaves of Grass* that I proposed to bring out at the right time as a sort of certificate of character. But when that little girl jerked me right-about-face and heartlessly deserted me, I stared dumbly at the man whom I had come a hundred miles to see. I began angling for my little speech but could not fetch it.

"Hello!" called the philosopher, out of the white aureole ; "Hello! come here, boy!"

He held out his hand and as I took it there was a grasp with meaning in it.

"Don't go yet, Joe," he said to a man seated on the step smoking a cob pipe.

"The old woman's calling me," said the swarthy Joe. Joe evidently held truth lightly. "So long, Walt!"

"Good-bye, Joe. Sit down, lad, sit down!"

I sat in the doorway at his feet.

"Now is n't it queer—that fellow is a regular philosopher and works out some great problems, but he 's ashamed to express 'em. He could no more give you his best than he could fly. Ashamed I s'pose, ashamed of the best that is in him. We are all a little that way — all but me—I try to write my best, regardless of whether the thing sounds ridiculous or not—regardless of what others think or say or have said. Ashamed of our holiest, truest, and best ! Is it not too bad ?

" You are twenty-five now? well boy, you may grow until you are thirty and then you will be as wise as you ever will be. Have n't you noticed that men of sixty have no clearer vision than men of forty? One reason is that we have been taught that we know all about life and death and the mysteries of the grave. But the main reason is that we are ashamed to shove out and be ourselves. Jesus expressed his own individuality perhaps more than any man we know of, and so he wields a wider influence than any other. And this though we only have a record of just twenty-seven days of his life.

"Now that fellow that just left is an engineer, and he dreams some beautiful dreams, but he never expresses them to any one, only hints them to me, and this only at twilight. He is like a weasel or mink or a whip-poor-will, he comes out only at night.

"'If the weather was like this all the time people would never learn to read and write,' said Joe to me just as you arrived. And isn't that so? Here we can count a hundred people up and down this street, and not one is reading, not one but that is just lolling about, except the children and they are only happy when playing in the dirt. Why if this tropical weather should continue we would all slip back into South Sea Islanders! You can only raise good men in a little strip around the North Temperate Zone—when you get

out of the track of the glacier a tender
hearted, sympathetic man of brains is an
accident."

Then the old man suddenly ceased and
I imagined that he was following the
thought out in his own mind. We sat
silent for a space. The twilight fell, and
a lamp-lighter lit the street lamp on the
corner. He stopped an instant to cheerily
salute the poet as he past. The man sitting on the doorstep, across the street,
smoking, knocked the ashes out of his
pipe on his boot heel and went indoors.
Women called their children, who did
not respond, but still played on. Then
the creepers were carried in, to be fed
their bread and milk and put to bed ; and
shortly shrill feminine voices ordered the
older children indoors, and some obeyed.

The night crept slowly on.

I heard old Walt chuckle behind me,
talking incoherently to himself, and then
he said :

"You are wondering why I live in
such a place as this?"

"Yes, that is exactly what I was thinking of!"

"You think I belong in the country, in
some quiet shady place. But all I have
to do is to shut my eyes and go there.
No man loves the woods more than I—I
was born within sound of the sea—down
on Long Island and I know all the songs
that the sea-shell sings. But this babble
and babel of voices pleases me better
especially since my legs went on a strike,
for although I can't walk, you see I still
mix with the throng, so I suffer no loss.
In the woods a man must be all hands
and feet. I like the folks, the plain,
ignorant unpretentious folks; and the
youngsters that come and slide on my
cellar door do not disturb me a bit. I'm
different from Carlyle—you know he had
a noise-proof room where he locked himself in. Now when a huckster goes by,
crying his wares I open the blinds, and
often wrangle with the fellow over the
price of things. But the rogues have got
into a way lately of leaving truck for me

and refusing pay. To-day an Irishman passed in three quarts of berries and walked off pretending to be mad because I offered to pay. When he was gone, I beckoned to the babies over the way— they came over and we had a feast.

"Yes, I like the folks around here; I like the women, and I like the men, and I like the babies, and I like the youngsters that play in the alley and make mud pies on my steps. I expect to stay here until I die."

"You speak of death as a matter of course—you are not afraid to die?"

"Oh, no, my boy, death is as natural as life, and a deal kinder. But it is all good—I accept it all and give thanks— you have not forgotten my chant to death?"

"Not I!"

I repeated a few lines from *Drum Taps*.

He followed me, rapping gently with his cane on the floor, and with little interjectory remarks of "That's so!" "Very true!" "Good, good!" And

when I faltered and lost the lines he
picked them up where " The voice of
my spirit tallied the song of the bird."
In a strong clear voice but a voice full
of sublime feeling he repeated :

Come, lovely and soothing Death,
Undulate round the world, serenely arriving,
    arriving,
In the day, in the night, to all, to each,
Sooner or later, delicate Death.
Praised be the fathomless universe
For life and joy, and for objects and knowledge
    curious,
And for love, sweet love—but praise ! praise !
    praise
For the sure enwinding arms of cool, enfolding
    Death.
Dark Mother, always gliding near with soft feet,
Have none chanted for thee a chant of fullest
    welcome ?
Then I chant for thee, I glorify thee above all,
I bring thee a song that when thou must indeed
    come, come unfalteringly
Approach, strong deliveress,
When it is so, when thou hast taken them
I joyously sing the dead,
Lost in the loving, floating ocean of thee,
Laved in the flood of thy bliss, O Death.
From me to thee glad serenades,
Dances for thee I propose, saluting thee, adorn-
    ments and feastings for thee,
And the sights of the open landscape and the
    high spread sky are fitting,
And life and the fields, and the huge and thought-
    ful night.

The night in silence under many a star,
The ocean shore and the husky whispering
    wave whose voice I know,
And the soul turning to thee, O vast and well
    veil'd Death,
And the body gratefully nestling close to thee.
Over the tree-tops I float thee a song,
Over the rising and sinking waves, over the
    myriad fields and the prairies wide,
Over the dense-packed cities all, and the teem-
    ing wharves, and ways,
I float this carol with joy, with joy to thee O
    Death.

The last playing youngster had silently
disappeared from the streets. The doorsteps were deserted—save where across the
way a young man and maiden sat in the
gloaming conversing in low monotone.

The clouds had drifted away.

A great yellow star shone out above the
chimney tops in the east.

I arose to go.

"I wish you'd come oftener—I see you
so seldom, lad," said the old man, half
plaintively.

I did not explain that we had never
met before—that I had come from New
York purposely to see him. He thought
he knew me. And so he did—as much

as I could impart. The rest was irrelevant. As to my occupation or name, what booted it?—he had no curiosity concerning me. I grasped his outstretched hand in both of my own.

He said not a word; neither did I.

I turned and made my way to the ferry—past the whispering lovers on the doorsteps, and over the railway tracks where the noisy engines puffed. As I walked on board the boat the wind blew up cool and fresh from the west. The star in the east grew brighter, and other stars came out, reflecting themselves like gems in the dark blue of the Delaware.

There was a soft sublimity in the sound of the bells that came echoing over the waters. My heart was very full for I had felt the thrill of being in the presence of a great and loving soul.

It was the first time and the last that I ever saw Walt Whitman.

III.

MOST writers bear no message : they carry no torch. Sometimes they excite wonder, or they amuse and divert—divert us from our work. To be diverted to a certain degree may be well, but there is a point where earth ends and cloudland begins, and even great poets occasionally befog the things which they would reveal.

Homer was seemingly blind to much simple truth ; Virgil carries you away from earth ; Horace was undone without his Macænas ; Dante makes you an exile ; Shakespeare was singularly silent concerning the doubts, difficulties, and common lives of common people ; Byron's Corsair life does not help you in your toil, and in his fight with English Bards and Scotch Reviewers we crave neutrality; to be caught in the meshes of Pope's *Dunciad* is not pleasant; and Lowell's *Fable for Critics* is only another *Dunciad*. But above all poets who have ever lived the author of *Leaves of Grass* was the poet of humanity.

Milton knew all about Heaven, and Dante conducts us through Hell, but it was left for Whitman to show us Earth. His voice never goes so high that it breaks an impotent falsetto, neither does it growl and snarl at things it does not understand and not understanding does not like. He was so great that he had no envy, and his insight was so sure that he had no prejudice. He never boasted that he was higher, nor claimed to be less than any of the other sons of men. He met all on terms of absolute equality, mixing with the poor, the lowly, the fallen, the oppressed, the cultured, the rich—simply as brother with brother. And when he said to the outcast, "Not till the sun excludes you will I exclude you," he voiced a sentiment worthy of a god.

He was brother to the elements, the mountains, the seas, the clouds, the sky. He loved them all and partook of them all in his large, free, unselfish, untrammelled nature. His heart knew no limits, and feeling his feet mortis'd in granite and his footsteps tenon'd in infinity he knew the amplitude of time.

Only the great are generous; only the strong are forgiving. Like Lot's wife, most poets look back over their shoulders; and those who are not looking backward insist that we shall look into the future, and the vast majority of the whole scribbling rabble accept the precept, "Man never is, but always to be blest."

We grieve for childhood's happy days, and long for sweet rest in Heaven and sigh for mansions in the skies. And the people about us seem so indifferent, and our friends so lukewarm; and really no one understands us, and our environment queers our budding spirituality and the frost of jealousy nips our aspirations: "O Paradise, O Paradise, the world is growing old; who would not be at rest and free where love is never cold." So sing the fearsome dyspeptics of the stylus. O anæmic he, you bloodless she, nipping at crackers, sipping at tea, why not consider that although the evolutionists tell us where we came from, and the theologians inform us where we are going to, yet the only thing we are really sure of is that we are here!

The present is the perpetuality moving spot where history ends and prophecy begins. It is our only possession: the past we reach through lapsing memory, halting recollection, hearsay, and belief; we pierce the future by wistful faith or anxious hope, but the present is beneath our feet.

Whitman sings the beauty and the glory of the present. He rebukes our groans and sighs—bids us look about on every side at the wonders of creation, and at the miracles within our grasp. He lifts us up, restores us to our own, introduces us to man and Nature and thus infuses into us courage, manly pride, self-reliance, and the strong faith that comes when we feel our kinship with God.

He was so mixed with the universe that his voice took on the sway of elemental integrity and candor. Absolutely honest, this man was unafraid and unashamed, for Nature has neither apprehension, shame nor vain-glory. In *Leaves of Grass* Whitman speaks as all men have ever spoken who believe in God and in themselves—oracular, without apology, without abasement—fearlessly. He tells of the powers and mysteries that pervade and guide all life, all death, all purpose. His work is masculine, as the sun is masculine ; for the Prophetic voice is as surely masculine as the lullaby and lyric cry is feminine.

Whitman brings the warmth of the sun to the buds of the heart so that they open and bring forth form, color, perfume. He becomes for them aliment and dew ; so these buds become blossoms, fruits, tall branches, and stately trees that cast refreshing shadows.

There are men who are to other men as the shadow of a mighty rock in a weary land—such is Walt Whitman.

NATHANIEL HAWTHORNE

" It was sometimes the case," continued Grandfather, "that affrays happened between such
wild young men as these and small parties of the
soldiers. No weapons had hitherto been used
except fists or cudgels. But when men have
loaded muskets in their hands, it is easy to foretell that they will soon be turned against the
bosoms of those who provoke their anger."

" Grandfather," said little Alice, looking fearfully into his face, " your voice sounds as though
you were going to tell us something awful ! "

Grandfather's Chair.

198

NATHANIEL HAWTHORNE

BY GEORGE WILLIAM CURTIS.[*]

HAWTHORNE has himself drawn the picture of the "Old Manse" in Concord. He has given to it that quiet richness of coloring which ideally belongs to an old country mansion. It seems so fitting a residence for one who loves to explore the twilight of antiquity—and the gloomier the better—that the visitor, among the felicities of whose life was included the freedom of the Manse, could not but fancy that our author's eyes first saw the daylight enchanted by the slumberous orchard be-

[*] Written in 1853 for Putnam's *Homes of Ameri-can Authors*.

hind the house, or tranquillized into twilight by the spacious avenue in front. The character of his imagination, and the golden gloom of its blossoming, completely harmonize with the rusty, gable-roofed old house upon the river side, and the reader of his books would be sure that his boyhood and youth knew no other friends than the dreaming river, and the melancholy meadows and drooping foliage of its vicinity.

Since the reader, however, would greatly mistake if he fancied this, in good sooth, the ancestral halls of the Hawthornes,—the genuine Hawthornden,—he will be glad to save the credit of his fancy by knowing that it was here our author's bridal tour,—which commenced in Boston, then three hours away,—ended, and his married life began. Here, also, his first child was born, and here those sad and silver mosses accumulated upon his fancy, from which he heaped so soft a bed for our dreaming. "Between two tall gate-posts of rough hewn stone (the gate itself having fallen from its hinges at some unknown epoch) we beheld the gray front of the old parsonage, terminating the vista of an avenue of black ash trees." It was a pleasant spring day in the year 1843, and as they entered the house, nosegays of fresh flowers, arranged by friendly hands, welcomed them to Concord and summer.

The dark-haired man, who led his wife along the avenue that afternoon, had been recently an officer of the customs in Boston, before which he had led a solitary life in Salem. Graduated with Longfellow at Bowdoin College, in Maine, he had lived a hermit in respectable Salem, an absolute recluse even from his own family, walking out by night and writing wild tales by day, most of which were burnt in his bachelor fire, and some of which, in newspapers, magazines, and annuals, led a wandering, uncertain, and mostly unnoticed life. Those tales, among this class, which were attainable, he collected into a small volume, and apprising the world that they were "twice-told," sent them forth anew to make their own way, in the year 1841. But he piped to the world, and it did not dance. He wept to it, and it did not mourn. The book, however, as all good books do, made its way into various hearts. Yet the few penetrant minds which recognized a remarkable power and a method of strange fascination in the stories, did not make the public, nor influence the public mind. "I was," he says in the last edition of these tales, "the most unknown author in America." Full of glancing wit, of tender satire, of exquisite natural deception, of subtle and strange analysis of human life, darkly passionate and weird, they yet floated unhailed barques upon the sea of publicity, —unhailed, but laden and gleaming at every crevice with the true treasure of Cathay.

Bancroft, then Collector in Boston, prompt to recognize and to honor talent, made the dreaming story-teller a

surveyor in the custom-house, thus opening to him a new range of experience.
From the society of phantoms he stepped
upon Long Wharf and plumply con-
fronted Captain Cuttle and Dirck Hatteraick. It was no less romance to our
author. There is no greater error of
those who are called "practical men,"
than the supposition that life is, or can
be, other than a dream to a dreamer.
Shut him up in a counting-room, barricade him with bales of merchandise and
limit his library to the leger and cash-
book, and his prospect to the neighboring
signs; talk "Bills receivable" and "Sun-
dries Dr. to Cash" to him forever, and
you are only a very amusing or very
annoying phantom to him. The merchant prince might as well hope to make
himself a poet, as the poet a practical or
practicable man. He has laws to obey
not at all the less stringent because men
of a different temperament refuse to acknowledge them, and he is held to a
loyalty quite beyond their conceptions.

So Captain Cuttle and Dirck Hatteraick were as pleasant figures to our author in the picture of life, as any others. He went daily upon the vessels, looked, and listened, and learned ; was a favorite of the sailors, as such men always are,—did his work faithfully, and having dreamed his dream upon Long Wharf, was married and slipped up to the Old Manse, and a new chapter in the romance. It opened in "the most delightful little nook of a study that ever offered its snug seclusion to a scholar." Of the three years in the Old Manse the prelude to the *Mosses* is the most perfect history, and of the quality of those years the " Mosses " themselves are sufficient proof. They were mostly written in the little study, and originally published in the *Democratic Review*, then edited by Hawthorne's friend O'Sullivan.

To the inhabitants of Concord, however, our author was as much a phantom and a fable as the old Pastor of the parish, dead half a century before, and whose faded portrait in the attic was gradually rejoining its original in native dust. The gate, fallen from its hinges in a remote antiquity, was never re-hung. The wheel-track leading to the door remained still overgrown with grass. No bold villager ever invaded the sleep of the glimmering shadows in the avenue. At evening no lights gleamed from the windows. Scarce once in many months did the single old knobby-faced coachman at the railroad bring a fare to "Mr. Hawthorne's." "*Is* there anybody in the old house?" sobbed the old ladies in despair, imbibing tea of a livid green. The knocker, which everybody had enjoyed the right of lifting to summon the good old Pastor, no temerity now dared touch. Heavens! what if the figure in the mouldy portrait should peer, in answer, over the eaves, and shake solemnly his decaying surplice! Nay, what if the mysterious man himself should answer the summons and come to the door! It is easy to summon spirits,

—but if they come ? Collective Concord, mowing in the river meadows, embraced the better part of valor and left the knocker untouched. A cloud of romance suddenly fell out of the heaven of fancy and enveloped the Old Manse :

> In among the bearded barley
> The reaper reaping late and early

did not glance more wistfully toward the island of Shalott and its mysterious lady than the reapers of Concord rye looked at the Old Manse and wondered over its inmate.

Sometimes, in the forenoon, a darkly clad figure was seen in the little garden-plot putting in corn or melon seed, and gravely hoeing. It was a brief apparition. The farmer passing toward town and seeing the solitary cultivator, lost his faith in the fact and believed he had dreamed, when, upon returning, he saw no sign of life, except, possibly, upon some Monday, the ghostly skirt of a shirt flapping spectrally in the distant orchard. Day dawned and darkened over the lonely house. Summer with "buds and bird-voices" came singing in from the South, and clad the old ash trees in deeper green, the Old Manse, in profounder mystery. Gorgeous autumn came to visit the story-teller in his little western study, and departing, wept rainbows among his trees. Winter impatiently swept down the hill opposite, rifling the trees of each last clinging bit of Summer, as if thrusting aside opposing barriers and determined to search the mystery. But his white robes floated around the Old Manse, ghostly as the decaying surplice of the old Pastor's portrait, and in the snowy seclusion of Winter the mystery was as mysterious as ever.

Occasionally Emerson, or Ellery Channing, or Henry Thoreau,—some Poet, as once Whittier, journeying to the Merrimac, or an old Brook Farmer who remembered Miles Coverdale, with Arcadian sympathy,—went down the avenue and disappeared in the house. Sometimes a close observer, had he been ambushed among the long grasses of the orchard, might have seen the host and one of his guests emerging at the back door, and sauntering to the river-side, step into the boat, and float off until they faded in the shadow. The spectacle would not have lessened the romance. If it were afternoon,—one of the spectrally sunny afternoons which often bewitch that region,—he would be only the more convinced that there was something inexplicable in the whole matter of this man whom nobody knew, who was never once seen at town-meeting, and concerning whom it was whispered that he did not constantly attend church all day, although he occupied the reverend parsonage of the village, and had unmeasured acres of manuscript sermons in his attic, beside the nearly extinct portrait of an utterly extinct clergyman. Mrs. Radcliffe and Monk Lewis were nothing to this; and the awe-stricken observer, if he could creep safely out of the long grass, he did not fail to do so quietly, fortifying his courage by remembering stories of the genial humanity of the last old Pastor who inhabited the Manse, and who for fifty years was the bland and beneficent Pope of Concord. A genial, gracious old man, whose memory is yet sweet in the village, and who, wedded to the grave traditions of New England theology, believed of his young relative, Waldo Emerson, as Miss Flite, touching her forehead, said of her landlord, that he was "—M—quite—M—," but was proud to love in him the hereditary integrity of noble ancestors.

This old gentleman,—an eminent figure in the history of the Manse, and in all reminiscences of Concord,—partook sufficiently of mundane weaknesses to betray his mortality. Hawthorne describes him watching the battle of Concord, from his study window. But when the uncertainty of that dark moment had so happily resulted, and the first battle-ground of the Revolution had become a spot of hallowed and patriotic consideration, it was a pardonable pride in the good old man to order his servant, whenever there was company, to assist him in reaping the glory due to the owner of a spot so sacred. Accordingly, when some reverend or distinguished guest sat with the Pastor in his little parlor, or, of a summer evening, at the hospitable door under the trees, Jeremiah or Nicodemus, the cow-boy, would deferentially approach and inquire:

"Into what pasture shall I turn the cow to-night, Sir?"

And the old gentleman would audibly reply:

"Into the battle-field, Nicodemus, into the battle-field!"

Then naturally followed wonder, inquiry, a walk in the twilight to the river-bank, the old gentleman's story, the corresponding respect of the listening visitor, and the consequent quiet complacency and harmless satisfaction in the clergyman's bosom. That throb of pride was the one drop of peculiar advantage

which the Pastor distilled from the revolution. He could not but fancy that he
had a hand in so famous a deed accomplished upon land now his own, and de-
meaned himself, accordingly, with conti-
nental dignity.

The pulpit, however, was his especial
sphere. There he reigned supreme ; there
he exhorted, rebuked, and advised, as in
the days of Mather. There he inspired
that profound reverence, of which he was
so proud, and which induced the matrons
of the village, when he was coming to
make a visit, to bedizen the children in
their Sunday suits, to parade the best
tea-pot, and to offer the most capacious
chair. In the pulpit he delivered everything with the pompous cadence of the
elder New England clergy, and a sly joke
is told at the expense of his even temper,
that on one occasion, when loftily reading the hymn, he encountered a blot upon
the page quite obliterating the word,
but without losing the cadence, although
in a very vindictive tone at the truant

word, or the culprit who erased it,—he
finished the reading as follows :

> He sits upon the throne above,
>   Attending angels bless,
>   While Justice, Mercy, Truth, and—(an-
> other word which is blotted out)
>   Compose his princely dress.

We linger around the old Manse and
its occupants as fondly as Hawthorne,
but no more fondly than all who have
been once within the influence of its
spell.   There glimmers in my memory a
few hazy days, of a tranquil and half-pen-
sive character, which I am conscious were
passed in and around the house, and their
pensiveness I know to be only that touch
of twilight which inhered in the house
and its associations. Beside the few
chance visitors I have named, there were
city friends, occasionally, figures quite
unknown to the village, who came preceded by the steam-shriek of the locomotive, were dropped at the gate-posts, and
were seen no more. The owner was as
much a vague name to me as any one.

During Hawthorne's first year's resi-

dence in Concord, I had driven up with
some friends to an æsthetic tea at Mr.
Emerson's. It was in the winter and a
great wood-fire blazed upon the hospitable hearth. There were various men
and women of note assembled, and I,
who listened attentively to all the fine
things that were said, was for some time
scarcely aware of a man who sat upon
the edge of the circle, a little withdrawn,
his head slightly thrown forward upon
his breast, and his bright eyes clearly
burning under his black brow. As I
drifted down the stream of talk, this person, who sat silent as a shadow, looked
to me, as Webster might have looked had
he been a poet,—a kind of poetic Webster. He rose and walked to the window, and stood quietly there for a long
time, watching the dead white landscape.
No appeal was made to him, nobody
looked after him, the conversation flowed
steadily on as if everyone understood
that his silence was to be respected. It
was the same thing at table. In vain the

silent man imbibed æsthetic tea.   Whatever fancies it inspired did not flower at his lips.   But there was a light in his eye which assured me that nothing was lost. So supreme was his silence that it presently engrossed me to the exclusion of everything else.   There was very brilliant discourse, but this silence was much more poetic and fascinating.   Fine things were said by the philosophers, but much finer things were implied by the dumbness of this gentleman with heavy brows and black hair.   When he presently rose and went, Emerson, with the "slow, wise smile" that breaks over his face like day over the sky, said :

"Hawthorne rides well his horse of the night."

Thus he remained in my memory, a shadow, a phantom, until more than a year afterward.   Then I came to live in Concord.   Every day I passed his house, but when the villagers, thinking that perhaps I had some clue to the mystery, said :

"Do you know this Mr. Hawthorne?"
I said: "No," and trusted to Time.

Time justified my confidence and one day I, too, went down the avenue, and disappeared in the house. I mounted those mysterious stairs to that apocryphal study. I saw "the cheerful coat of paint, and golden-tinted paper-hangings, lighting up the small apartment; while the shadow of a willow tree, that swept against the overhanging eaves, atempered the cheery western sunshine." I looked from the little northern window whence the old Pastor watched the battle, and in the small dining-room beneath it, upon the first floor there were

Dainty chicken, snow-white bread,

and the golden juices of Italian vineyards, which still feast insatiable memory."

Our author occupied the Old Manse for three years. During that time he was not seen probably, by more than a dozen of the villagers. His walks could

easily avoid the town, and upon the river
he was always sure of solitude. It was
his favorite habit to bathe every evening
in the river, after nightfall, and in that
part of it over which the old bridge
stood, at which the battle was fought.
Sometimes, but rarely, his boat accompanied another up the stream, and I recall the silent and preternatural vigor
with which, on one occasion, he wielded
his paddle to counteract the bad rowing
of a friend who conscientiously considered it his duty to do something and not
let Hawthorne work alone; but who,
with every stroke, neutralized all Hawthorne's efforts. I suppose he would
have struggled until he fell senseless
rather than ask his friend to desist. His
principle seemed to be, if a man cannot
understand without talking to him, it is
quite useless to talk, because it is imma-
terial whether such a man understands
or not. His own sympathy was so broad
and sure, that although nothing had been
said for hours, his companion knew that

not a thing had escaped his eye, nor had a single pulse of beauty in the day, or scene, or society, failed to thrill his heart. In this way his silence was most social. Everything seemed to have been said. It was a Barmecide feast of discourse, from which a greater satisfaction resulted than from an actual banquet.

When a formal attempt was made to desert this style of conversation, the result was ludicrous. Once Emerson and Thoreau arrived to pay a call. They were shown into the little parlor upon the avenue, and Hawthorne presently entered. Each of the guests sat upright in his chair like a Roman senator; to them, Hawthorne, like a Dacian king. The call went on, but in a most melancholy manner. The host sat perfectly still, or occasionally propounded a question which Thoreau answered accurately, and there the thread broke short off. Emerson delivered sentences that only needed the setting of an essay to charm the world; but the whole visit was a vague ghost of the Monday Evening Club at Mr. Emerson's,—it was a great failure. Had they all been lying idly upon the river brink, or strolling in Thoreau's blackberry pastures, the result would have been utterly different. But imprisoned in the proprieties of a parlor, each a wild man in his way, with a necessity of talking inherent in the nature of the occasion, there was only a waste of treasure. This was the only "call" in which I ever knew Hawthorne to be involved.

In Mr. Emerson's house, I said it seemed always morning. But Hawthorne's black-ash trees and scraggy apple-boughs shaded "A land in which it seemed always afternoon." I do not doubt that the lotus grew along the grassy marge of the Concord behind his house, and that it was served, subtly concealed, to all his guests. The house, its inmates, and its life, lay, dream-like, upon the edge of the little village. You fancied that they all came together, and were glad that at length some idol of

your imagination, some poet whose spell
had held you, and would hold you, for
ever, was housed as such a poet should be.

During the lapse of the three years
since the bridal tour of twenty miles
ended at the "two tall gate-posts of rough
hewn stone," a little wicker wagon had
appeared at intervals upon the avenue,
and a placid babe, whose eyes the soft
Concord day had touched with the blue
of its beauty, lay looking tranquilly up
at the grave old trees, which sighed lofty
lullabies over her sleep. The tranquillity
of the golden-haired Una was the living
and breathing type of the dreamy life of
the old Manse. Perhaps, that being attained, it was as well to go. Perhaps our
author was not surprised nor displeased
when the hints came, "growing more
and more distinct, that the owner of the
old house was pining for his native air."
One afternoon I entered the study, and
learned from its occupant that the last
story he should ever write there was
written. The son of the old pastor yearned

for his homestead. The light of another summer would seek its poet in the Old Manse, but in vain.

While Hawthorne had been quietly writing in the "most delightful nook of a study," Mr. Polk had been elected President, and Mr. Bancroft in the Cabinet did not forget his old friend the surveyor in the custom-house. There came suggestions and offers of various attractions. Still loving New England, would he tarry there, or, as inspector of woods and forests in some far-away island of the Southern Sea, some hazy strip of distance seen from Florida, would he taste the tropics? He meditated all the chances, without immediately deciding. Gathering up his household gods, he passed out of the Old Manse as its heir entered, and before the end of summer was domesticated in the custom-house of his native town of Salem. This was in the year 1846.

Upon leaving the Old Manse he published the *Mosses*, announcing that it was the last collection of tales he should put forth. Those who knew him and recognized his value to our literature, trembled lest this was the last word from one who spoke only pearls and rubies. It was a foolish fear. The sun must shine—the sea must roll—the bird must sing, and the poet write. During his life in Salem, of which the introduction to the *Scarlet Letter* describes the official aspect, he wrote that romance. It is inspired by the spirit of the place. It presents more vividly than any history the gloomy picturesqueness of early New England life. There is no strain in our literature so characteristic or more real than that which Hawthorne had successfully attempted in several of his earlier sketches, and of which the *Scarlet Letter* is the great triumph. It became immediately popular, and directly placed the writer of stories for a small circle among the world's masters of romance.

Times meanwhile changed, and Presidents with them. General Tyler was

elected, and the Salem Collector retired.
It is one of the romantic points of Hawthorne's quiet life, that its changes have
been so frequently determined by political events, which, of all others, are the
most entirely foreign to his tastes and
habits. He retired to the hills of Berkshire, the eye of the world now regard-
ing his movements. There he lived a
year or two in a little red cottage upon
the "Stockbridge Bowl," as a small lake
near that town is called. In this retreat
he wrote the *House of the Seven Gables*,
which more deeply confirmed the literary
position already acquired for him by the
first romance. The scene is laid in Salem,
as if he could not escape a strange fascination in the witch-haunted town of our
early history. It is the same black canvas upon which plays the rainbow-flash
of his fancy, never, in its brightest moment, more than illuminating the gloom.
This marks all his writings. They have
a terrible beauty, like the Siren, and their
fascination is sure.

Nathaniel Hawthorne

After six years of absence, Hawthorne has returned to Concord, where he has purchased a small house formerly occupied by Orphic Alcott. When that philosopher came into possession, it was a miserable house of two peaked gables. But the genius which recreated itself in devising graceful summer-houses, like that for Mr. Emerson, already noticed, soon smoothed the new residence into some kind of comeliness. It was an old house when Mr. Alcott entered it, but his tasteful finger touched it with picturesque grace. Not like a tired old drudge of a house, rusting into unhonored decay, but with a modest freshness that does not belie the innate sobriety of a venerable New England farm-house, the present residence of our author stands withdrawn a few yards from the high road to Boston, along which marched the British soldiers to Concord bridge. It lies at the foot of a wooded hill, a neat house of a "rusty olive hue," with a porch in front, and a central peak and a

piazza at each end. The genius for summer-houses has had full play upon the
hill behind. Here, upon the homely
steppes of Concord, is a strain of Persia.
Mr. Alcott built terraces, and arbors, and
pavilions, of boughs and rough stems of
trees, revealing—somewhat inadequately,
perhaps—the hanging gardens of delight
that adorn the Babylon of his Orphic
imagination. The hill-side is no unapt
emblem of his intellectual habit, which
garnishes the arid commonplaces of life
with a cold poetic aurora, forgetting that
it is the inexorable law of light to de-
form as well as adorn. Treating life as a
grand epic poem, the philosopher Alcott
forgets that Homer must nod, or we
should all fall asleep. The world would
not be very beautiful nor interesting, if it
were all one huge summit of Mont Blanc.

Unhappily, the terraced hill-side, like
the summer-house upon Mr. Emerson's
lawn, "lacks technical arrangement,"
and the wild winds play with these architectural toys of fancy, like lions with

Truly Yours,

Nath¹ Hawthorne

Concord, July 15th '52.

I passed by the Old Manse, a few days ago, for the first time in nearly seven years. Notwithstanding the repairs, it looked very much as of yore; except that a large window had been opened on the roof, through which light and cheerfulness probably shine into the darkest part of the dim garret of my own time. The trees of the avenue — how many leaves have fallen since I last saw them! — had an aspect of non-freshness, which disappointed me; either

Truly Yours,
Nat'l Hawthorne

FACSIMILE PAGE OF LETTER OF HAWTHORNE.

humming-birds. They are gradually falling, shattered,—and disappearing. Fine locust-trees shade them, and ornament the hill with perennial beauty. The hanging gardens of Semiramis were not more fragrant than Hawthorne's hill-side during the June blossoming of the locusts. A few young elms, some white pines and young oaks complete the catalogue of trees. A light breeze constantly fans the brow of the hill, making harps of the tree-tops, and singing to our author, who "with a book in my hand, or an unwritten book in my thoughts," lies stretched beneath them in the shade.

From the height of the hill the eye courses, unrestrained, over the solitary landscape of Concord, broad and still, broken only by the slight wooded undulations of insignificant hillocks. The river is not visible, nor any gleam of lake. Walden Pond is just behind the wood in front, and not far away over the meadows sluggishly steals the river. It is the most quiet of prospects. Eight acres of good land lie in front of the house, across the road, and in the rear the estate extends a little distance over the brow of the hill.

This latter is not good garden-ground, but it yields that other crop which the poet "gathers in a song." Perhaps the world will forgive our author that he is not a prize farmer, and makes but an indifferent figure at the annual cattle-show. We have seen that he is more nomadic than agricultural. He has wandered from spot to spot, pitching a temporary tent, then striking it for "fresh fields and pastures new." It is natural, therefore, that he should call his house "The Wayside,"—a bench upon the road where he sits for a while before passing on. If the wayfarer finds him upon that bench he shall have rare pleasure in sitting with him, yet shudder while he stays. For the pictures of our poet have more than the shadows of Rembrandt. If you listen to his story, the lonely pastures and dull towns of our dear old homely

New England shall become suddenly as radiant with grace and terrible with tragedy as any country and any time. The waning afternoon in Concord, in which the blue-frocked farmers are reaping and hoeing, shall set in pensive glory. The woods will forever after be haunted with strange forms. You will hear whispers, and music "i' the air." In the softest morning you will suspect sadness ; in the most fervent noon, a nameless terror. It is because the imagination of our author treads the almost imperceptible line between the natural and the supernatural. We are all conscious of striking it sometimes. But we avoid it. We recoil and hurry away, nor dare to glance over our shoulders lest we should see phantoms. What are these tales of supernatural appearances, as well authenticated as any news of the day,—and what is the sphere which they imply? What is the more subtle intellectual apprehension of fate and its influence upon imagination and life? Whatever it is, it is the mystery of the fascination of these tales. They converse with that dreadful realm as with our real world. The light of our sun is poured by genius upon the phantoms we did not dare to contemplate, and lo? they are ourselves, unmasked, and playing our many parts. An unutterable sadness seizes the reader, as the inevitable black thread appears. For here Genius assures us what we trembled to suspect, but could not avoid suspecting, that the black thread is inwoven with all forms of life, with all development of character.

It is for this peculiarity, which harmonizes so well with ancient places, whose pensive silence seems the trance of memory musing over the young and lovely life that illuminated its lost years,—that Hawthorne is so intimately associated with the "Old Manse." Yet that was but the tent of a night for him. Already with the *Blithedale Romance*, which is dated from Concord, a new interest begins to cluster around "The Wayside."

I know not how I can more fitly con-
clude these reminiscences of Concord and
Hawthorne, whose own stories have always a saddening close, than by relating
an occurrence which blighted to many
hearts the beauty of the quiet Concord
river, and seemed not inconsonant with
its lonely landscape. It has the further
fitness of typifying the operation of our
author's imagination : a tranquil stream,
clear and bright with sunny gleams,
crowned with lilies and graceful with
swaying grass, yet doing terrible deeds
inexorably, and therefore forever after,
of a shadowed beauty.

Martha was the daughter of a plain
Concord farmer, a girl of delicate and
shy temperament, who excelled so much
in study that she was sent to a fine academy in a neighboring town, and won all
the honors of the course. She met at
the school, and in the society of the
place, a refinement and cultivation, a
social gayety and grace, which were entirely unknown in the hard life she had

led at home, and which by their very
novelty, as well as because they harmo-
nized with her own nature and dreams,
were doubly beautiful and fascinating.
She enjoyed this life to the full, while
her timidity kept her only a spectator;
and she ornamented it with a fresher
grace, suggestive of the woods and fields,
when she ventured to engage in the airy
game. It was a sphere for her capacities
and talents. She shone in it, and the
consciousness of a true position and
genial appreciation gave her the full use
of all her powers. She admired and was
admired. She was surrounded by grati-
fications of taste, by the stimulants and
rewards of ambition. The world was
happy, and she was worthy to live in it.
But at times a cloud suddenly dashed
athwart the sun—a shadow stole, dark
and chill, to the very edge of the charmed
circle in which she stood. She knew well
what it was, and what it foretold, but she
would not pause nor heed. The sun
shone again; the future smiled; youth,

beauty, and all gentle hopes and thoughts bathed the moment in lambent light.

But school-days ended at last, and with the receding town in which they had been passed, the bright days of life disappeared, and forever. It is probable that the girl's fancy had been fed, perhaps indiscreetly pampered, by her experience there. But it was no fairy-land. It was an academy town in New England, and the fact that it was so alluring is a fair indication of the kind of life from which she had emerged, and to which she now returned. What could she do? In the dreary round of petty details, in the incessant drudgery of a poor farmer's household, with no companions of any sympathy—for the family of a hard-working New England farmer are not the Chloes and Clarissas of pastoral poetry, nor are cow-boys Corydons, —with no opportunity of retirement and cultivation, for reading and studying, which is always voted "stuff" under such circumstances,—the light suddenly

quenched out of life, what was she to
do?

" Adapt herself to her circumstances.
Why had she shot from her sphere in this
silly way? " demands unanimous com.
mon sense in valiant heroics.

The simple answer is, that she had
only used all her opportunities, and that,
although it was no fault of hers that the
routine of her life was in every way re-
pulsive, she did struggle to accommodate
herself to it,—and failed. When she
found it impossible to drag on at home,
she became an inmate of a refined and
cultivated household in the village, where
she had opportunity to follow her own
fancies, and to associate with educated
and attractive persons. But even here
she could not escape the feeling that it
was all temporary, that her position was
one of dependence; and her pride, now
grown morbid often drove her from the
very society which alone was agreeable
to her. This was all genuine. There
was not the slightest strain of the *femme*

incomprise in her demeanor. She was always shy and silent, with a touching reserve which won interest and confidence, but left also a vague sadness in the mind of the observer. After a few months she made another effort to rend the cloud which was gradually darkening around her, and opened a school for young children. But although the interest of friends secured for her a partial success, her gravity and sadness failed to excite the sympathy of her pupils, who missed in her the playful gayety always most winning to children. Martha, however, pushed bravely on, a figure of tragic sobriety to all who watched her course. The farmers thought her a strange girl, and wondered at the ways of a farmer's daughter who was not content to milk cows, and churn butter, and fry pork, without further hope or thought. The good clergyman of the town, interested in her situation, sought a confidence she did not care to bestow, and so, doling out *a*, *b*, *c*, to a wild group of boys and

---

girls, she found that she could not untie
the Gordian knot of her life, and felt,
with terror, that it must be cut.

One summer evening she left her
father's house and walked into the fields
alone. Night came, but Martha did not
return. The family became anxious,
inquired if anyone had noticed the direction in which she went, learned from
the neighbors that she was not visiting,
that there was no lecture nor meeting to
detain her, and wonder passed into apprehension. Neighbors went into the
adjacent woods and called, but received
no answer. Every instant the awful
shadow of some dread event solemnized
the gathering groups. Everyone thought
what no one dared to whisper, until a
low voice suggested "the river." Then,
with the swiftness of certainty, all friends,
far and near, were roused, and thronged
along the banks of the stream. Torches
flashed in boats that put off in the terrible
search. Hawthorne, then living in the
Old Manse, was summoned, and the man

whom the villagers had only seen at morning as a musing spectre in his garden, now appeared among them at night to devote his strong arm and steady heart to their service. The boats drifted slowly down the stream—the torches flared strangely upon the black repose of the water, and upon the long, slim grasses that, weeping, fringed the marge. Upon banks, silent and awe-stricken crowds hastened along, eager and dreading to find the slightest trace of what they sought. Suddenly they came upon a few articles of dress, heavy with the night dew. No one spoke, for no one had doubted the result. It was clear that Martha had strayed to the river, and quietly gained the repose she sought. The boats gathered round the spot. With every implement that could be of service the melancholy task began. Long intervals of fearful silence ensued, but at length, toward midnight, the sweet face of the dead girl was raised more

placidly to the stars than ever it had been
to the sun.

> Oh ! is it weed, or fish, or floating hair,—
>> A tress o' golden hair,
>> O' drownèd maiden's hair,
>> Above the nets at sea ?
> Was never salmon yet that shone so fair
>> Among the stakes on Dee.

So ended the village tragedy. The
reader may possibly find in it the original of the thrilling conclusion of the
Blithedale Romance, and learn anew
that dark as is the thread with which
Hawthorne weaves his spells, it is no
darker than those with which tragedies
are spun, even in regions apparently so
torpid as Concord.

AUDUBON

The aboriginal men who carried fire from a volcano and then after many centuries started a little blaze of their own did a mighty deed. But gorillas carry clubs, and apes throw stones, and certain varieties of woodpeckers play on musical instruments for the benefit of their mates, hunting long and carefully for a resonant piece of timber.

Lecture on Bird-Life.

AUDUBON.

BY PARKE GODWIN.*

ONE Sunday, as bright and brilliant a day as ever gladdened the eyesight, or sent thrilling pulses of health through the outworn body, I wandered, as it was then my habit, beyond the outskirts of New York. My road led me past several suburban houses, pleasantly rising amid their green groves, and along the banks of the Hudson. A sacred silence was brooding everywhere, as if Nature, sympathizing with the solemn offices of the day, had consecrated an hour to meditation. Behind me lay

* Written in 1853 for Putnam's *Homes of American Authors.*

the town with its masses of perpetual un-
quiet life ; before me the sloops with their
white wings were floating lazily on the
surface of the stream ; while all around
were the green fields and the cheering
sunshine. Those squads of strollers who
usually select that day for the invasion of
the sylvan solitudes, were not yet abroad,
and only the insects with their small hum,
or the birds with their sweet morning
hymns, seemed to be alive in the midst
of the infinite repose.

After wandering for some hours, I
turned into a rustic road which led directly down towards the river. A noble
forest was planted on one side of it, and
on the other vast grainfields lay laughing
in the sun, or listening to the complacent
murmur of a brook that stole along in
the midst of clumps of bushes and wild
briers. About the half-worn path groups
of cattle loitered, some cropping the
young grass, and others looking contem-
platively towards the distant shine of the
stream, which flashed through the vista

of trees in molten bands of silver. It was such a scene as Cuyp or Paul Potter would have loved to paint, if the native country of those artists had ever furnished them with so lovely and glorious a subject.

But my walk soon brought a secluded country house into view,—a house not entirely adapted to the nature of the scenery, yet simple and unpretending in its architecture, and beautifully embowered amid elms and oaks. Several graceful fawns and a noble elk were stalking in the shade of the trees, apparently unconscious of the presence of a few dogs, and not caring for the numerous turkeys, geese, and other domestic animals that gabbled and screamed around them. Nor did my own approach startle the wild, beautiful creatures that seemed as docile as any of their tame companions.

"Is the master at home?" I asked of a pretty maid-servant who answered my tap at the door, and who after informing me that he was, led me into a room on the left side of the broad hall. It was not, however, a parlor, or an ordinary reception-room that I entered, but evidently a room for work. In one corner stood a painter's easel, with a half-finished sketch of a beaver on paper; in the other lay the skin of an American panther. The antlers of elks hung upon the walls; stuffed birds of every description of gay plumage ornamented the mantle-piece; and exquisite drawings of field-mice, orioles, and woodpeckers were scattered promiscuously in other parts of the room, across one end of which a long rude table was stretched to hold artist materials, scraps of drawing paper, and immense folio volumes filled with delicious paintings of birds taken in their haunts.

This, said I to myself, is the studio of the naturalist, but hardly had the thought escaped me, when the master himself made his appearance. He was a tall, thin man, with a high arched and serene forehead, and a bright penetrating gray eye ; his white locks fell in clusters upon his shoulders, but were the only signs of age, for his form was erect, and his step as light as that of a deer. The expression of his face was sharp, but noble and commanding, and there was something in it, partly derived from the aquiline nose and partly from the shutting of the mouth, which made you think of the imperial eagle.

His greeting, as he entered, was at once frank and cordial, and showed you the sincere and true man. "How kind it is," he said with a slight French accent, and in a pensive tone, "to come to see me ; and how wise, too, to leave that crazy city !" He then shook me warmly by the hand. "Do you know," he continues, "how I wonder that men can consent to swelter and fret their lives away amid those hot bricks and pestilent vapors, when the woods and fields are all so near? It would kill me soon to be confined in such a prison-house ; and when I am forced to make an occasional visit there it fills me with loathing and sadness. Ah! how often when I have been abroad on the mountains 'has my heart risen in grateful praise to God that it was not my destiny to waste and pine among those noisome congregations of the city."

This man was Audubon, the ornithologist, whose extraordinary adventures in the pursuit of a favorite science, whose simple, manly character, and whose unequalled accuracy and skill as an artist in a peculiar walk, has made his name known to the civilized world.

He was over sixty years of age when the writer of this sketch made his acquaintance, and he was then as ardent in the prosecution of his studies, as bold in his projects for additional acquisitions, and as animated in his conversation and manner, as he could have been forty years before. Indeed, he was even at that advanced period of his life on the eve of an excursion to the Rocky Mountains, in search of some specimens of wild animals of which he had heard, and the following year he passed the summer on the Upper Missouri and the Yellowstone rivers. His love of his vocation, after innumerable trials, successes, and disappointments, gave the lie to the *Quo fit Macœnas* of Horace, and was to the end of his life most intense.

Audubon was born the same year the Declaration of Independence was made (1776), on a plantation in Louisiana, then a French possession, where his father, a retired and cultivated French naval officer, had settled, and where, under the instruction of that excellent parent, he acquired as a mere child his love for natural objects. As early as he could remember, he says, he took an interest in the animal creation, and because he could not be always with the birds, he brought the birds to him, as well as he could, by taking their portraits, in a rude uninstructed way.

The young naturalist was sent to France to perfect his skill. In Paris, he took lessons of David, but soon grew weary of the task, and longed to return once more to his native woods. "What had I to do," he asked, "with monstrous torsos and the heads of heathen gods, when my business lay among the birds?" Sure enough; and accordingly, the student made his way back to the fields. He took possession of a farm on the banks of the Schuyl-kill, in Pennsylvania, which had been given to him by his father, and here the taste thus early developed became the master passion of his life. He continued his researches and his drawings; but let it here be said, for the encouragement of youthful genius, that those drawings did not then display the excellence which marked his subsequent efforts.

It was not long after that he was married to a woman in every way adapted to his elevated taste,—one who appreciated his genius and sympathized in his pursuits; and with her, the better to pursue his studies, he removed to a residence he had purchased at Henderson, Kentucky.

He gives a graphic account of his first journey to that new home, which was then distant and desolate. Steamboats had not yet vexed the placid waters of the Ohio, to drive away the flat-boat and the canoe, and the shores were still covered with a luxuriant virgin vegetation. Unbroken thickets, enormous trees, endless reaches of forests rose on all sides, and where populous cities now send up their noise and smoke, the vultures screamed from the hill-tops, and savage animals came down to the openings to drink. But all this only made the region more inviting to the young voyager, and he penetrated the vast solitudes with a sprightly, eager joy. It was precisely amid the rich and varied magnificence of nature that he hoped to find those winged treasures for which his soul yearned. Creation in her fulness and glory was there, and he only longed to bathe in her luxuriance.

Once settled in his rustic Western dwelling, Audubon made wide and frequent excursions, not merely into all parts of the neighboring country, but over much of our whole broad inland. Provided with a rough leathern dress, with a knapsack that contained his pencils and colors, and with a good trusty gun at his side, he wandered for days, and even months, in search of animals to describe and paint. At one time, we find him watching for hours in the tangled canebreaks of Kentucky, where some shy songster is silently rearing her brood , at another, he is seen scaling the almost inaccessible mountains, where the eagle hovers over its rocky nest ; now he is floating in a frail skiff down the rushing tide of the Mississippi, and is carried on he knows not whither by the flood ; then the jealous Indian prowls about his lonely path, or lurks beneath the trees in which he sleeps, waiting for an opportunity to put an end to his life and his uncomprehended labors together ; here he begs shelter and food in some lonely log-cabin of the frontiers,—and there he wanders

hopelessly through the interminable pine-
barrens of Florida, while hunger and
heat and thirst, and insects and wild
beasts, beleaguer his steps like so many
persecuting spirits. But wherever he is,
whatever lot betides,—in difficulty and
danger, as well as in the glow of discov-
ery and success,—the same high, genial
enthusiasm warms him, the same unfaltering purpose sustains and fortifies his
soul. The hero on the battle-field never
marched to victory more firmly than he
marched to the conquests of science and
art. What opulent experiences, what
varieties and revulsions of feeling, what
dread despairs and exulting hopes were
involved in that long solitary career?
We fancy that we who live amid the incessant whirl of our straining civilization,
who are caught up and borne onward by
its manifold warring streams of trade,
politics, amusement, and frivolity, that
we know something of life ; but that
wandering naturalist, I take it, had ex-
citements in his lonely life to which our

strongest anxieties would be tame. The
spirit in solitude is brought face to face
with realities more awful and stern than
death, and therefore it is that the sea, the
desert, the still endless wood, when we
are alone with them, move our profoundest and saddest emotions.

It was curious to observe the influence
which this life had exerted upon the
mind and character of Audubon. With-
drawing him from the conventionalities
and cares of a more social condition, he
always retained the fresh, spontaneous,
elastic manner of a child, yet his constant
and deep conversation with the thoughtful mysteries of nature, had imparted to
him also the reflective wisdom of the
sage. Whatever came into his mind he
uttered with delightful unreserve and
naïvete ; but those utterances at the same
time bore marks of keen original insight,
and of the deepest knowledge. Thus,
he knew nothing of the theology of the
schools, and cared as little for it, because
the untaught theology of the woods had

filled his mind with a nobler sense of
God than the schoolmen had ever
dreamed ; he knew, too, nothing of our
politics, and cared nothing for them, because to his simple integrity they seemed
only frivolous and vain debates about
rights that none disputed, and duties that
all fulfilled : and his reading, confined, I
suspect, mainly to the necessary literature of his profession, was neither extensive nor choice, because he found in his
own activity, earnestness, and invention,
a fountain-head of literature, abundantly
able to supply all his intellectual and
spiritual wants.   The heroism and poetry
of his own life gave him no occasion to
learn the heroism and poetry of others ;
yet his apparent neglect of the " human-
ites " had wrought no hardening or vul-
garizing effect upon his nature, for his
sympathies were delicate, and his manners soft, gentle and refined.

After years of labor, some of his drawings were shown by him to Lawson, who
engraved designs for the works of Lucien

Bonaparte, Prince of Musignano, but they were rejected by Lawson as quite impossible to be engraved.

Nothing daunted by this repulse, Audubon at length proceeded to England. He relates with the utmost simplicity that on going to Europe, he trod its busy cities more desolate of heart amid their throngs than he had ever been in the woods, and fancied that no one of all the driving multitudes there, would know or care about the unfriended backwoodsman, who came without acquaintances and without introduction, to solicit their hospitality and aid. But what was his surprise and delight to find that at Edinburgh he was generously welcomed by Jeffrey, Wilson, and Sir Walter Scott; while at Paris, Cuvier, St. Hilaire, and Humboldt (whom, by the way, he had once casually met in America) were proud to call him friend. The learned societies hastened to greet him with their first academical honors, and he was introduced as a companion and peer among men

eminent in all walks of literature and art,
whose names are illustrious and venerable in both hemispheres. No painful
quarantine of hope deferred, as too often
falls to the lot of genius, was appointed
to his share,—no protracted poverty withered and cut short his labors. The result
was a work on Ornithology,—with splendid volumes of paintings, illustrated in
the letter-press with animated descriptions and lively incidents of personal
adventure. When it was published, it at
once established his fame abroad, and,
though he knew it not, gave him a high
reputation at home. But besides the
willing and instant applause he received,
it should be said that of the one hundred
and seventy subscribers to his book, at
one thousand dollars each, nearly half
came from England and France. This
testimony to his merit was as honorable
to those who gave it as it was to him who
received it, and must have largely com-
pensated him—not for the expense,
which we will not mention here—but for

the trouble and pain of his almost mirac-
ulous exertions.

After a few years he returned to America to enrich his portfolios and journals
with materials for other volumes of what
he characteristically named his "Ornith-
ological Biography." No term could have
been more happily chosen to designate
both his paintings and descriptions, for
both are actual histories of their objects.
A faithful portrait or transcript of the
form and plumage of his aerial friends
was not all that he desired to accomplish,
as if they had no lives of their own and
no relations to the rest of nature, and
sat for ever, melancholy and alone, like
the stock-dove of the poet, brooding over
their own sweet notes. He wished to portray them in their actual habitudes and
localities, such as he had found them for
years in their homes. Knowing how they
were reared and mated and made a living,
how each one had its individualities of
character and custom, how its motions
and postures and migrations were as

much a part of its history as its structure
and hue, and how the food it fed upon, as
well as the trees on which it built, were
important elements in the knowledge of
it, as a fact of creation, he strove to rep-
resent each in its most characteristic and
striking peculiarities and ways. And by
this means he obtained another end, beyond fidelity to the truth of things, in
that rich variety of accessories, which is
essential to picturesque effect.

This was not, however, a success that
in any degree intoxicated his mind, for
no sooner had he finally returned home,
crowned with fame and easy in fortune,
than he resumed his arduous tasks. His
was not a nature that could be content
with reposing upon laurels. On the con-
trary, an incessant activity was the law
of life. If anything could have tempted
him into the indolence of a comfortable
retirement, it was the charm of his happy
family, where, surrounded by his accomplished wife and sons, blessed with com-
petence, and enjoying general respect, he

could have whiled away the evenings of
his days in security, peace, and affection.
But stronger than these to him were the
seductions of the fields and that nameless
restless impulse which ever forces men
of genius along their peculiar paths. He
was soon again immersed in preparations
for his perilous journeys, and set out
upon them with as much hopefulness
and joy as had ever marked his earlier
days.

Those who have turned over the leaves
of Audubon's large books, or better still,
who remember to have seen the collected
exhibition he once made in the Lyceum
of this city, will recall with grateful feeling the advantages of his method. They
will remember how that vast and brilliant collection made it appear to the
spectator as if he had been admitted at
once to all sylvan secrets, or at least that
the gorgeous infinity of the bird-world
had been revealed to him in some happy
moment of nature's confidence. All the
gay denizens of the air were there,—some

alone on swaying twigs of the birch or
maple, or on bending ferns and spires of
grass ; others in pairs tenderly feeding
their young with gaudy or green insects,
or in groups pursuing their prey or de-
fending themselves from attack ; while
others again clove the thin air of the hills
or flitted darkly through secluded brakes.
All were alive,—all graceful,—all joyous.
It was impossible not to feel among them
that there was something in birds which
brought them nearer to our affection than
the rest of the animal tribes ; for while
these are either indifferent to us, or inimi-
cal, or mere servile ministers, birds are
ever objects of admiration and solicitude.
Nobody loves or even so much as likes
insects, or reptiles, or worms ; fishes
have an unutterably stupid and unsenti-
mental look, and deserve to be caught ;
wild beasts, though sometimes savagely
grand and majestic, are always dreadful,
and tame beasts we subjugate and therefore despise ; but birds win their way to
our hearts and imaginations by a thou-

saud ties. They are lovely in their forms and fascinating in their habits. They have canny knowing eyes, they have wonderfully pretty and brilliant hues, their motions are the perfection of beauty, and they lead free, happy, melodious lives. Their swift and graceful evolutions, now rising like an arrow to the very gate of heaven, and anon outspeeding the wind as it curls the white caps of the ocean, and above all, their faroff mysterious flights in the drear autumn, awaken aspirations and thought, and breed a vague mysterious human interest in their destinies, while their songs, profuse, varied, sparkling, sympathetic, glorious, filling the world with melody, are the richest and tenderest of nature's voices. Among the recollections of childhood, those of the birds we have fed and cherished are often the sweetest, and in maturer years the country home we love, the nooks where we have meditated, or the field in which we have worshipped, are the greener and the dearer for the memory of the birds. Thus they are associated with the most charming features of the external world, and breathe a spell over the interior world of thought. They are the poetry of nature, and at the same time a pervading presence of poetry. Shakspeare, Keats, Shelley, Burns, Bryant, and Wordsworth are their laureates, and while language lasts we shall hear an echo of their strains in the cadences of "immortal verse."

In this view of the matter, Audubon needs no apology for his lifelong devotion to birds, or for the affectionate interest he everywhere manifests in his writings about them. It must not be understood that he was exclusive in his attachments, for besides the nomenclature and scientific descriptions of his volumes, there are delightful episodes on natural scenery, local character and amusements, anecdotes of adventure, and sketches of the grander phenomena of winds and floods. In one place he tells us of an earthquake he experienced, in another of a fearful tempest, next of the hospitality of old friends suddenly and strangely found in a secluded corner of Canada, then of a ball in Newfoundland or of a barbecue iu Kentucky, and anon we are iuitiated into the mysteries of the maple-sugar camp, or stand appalled at the inhuman feats of the wreckers of the Florida reefs. His style, sometimes a little too ambitious and diffuse, is always vivacious and clear. The slight vein of egotism that runs through his interludes, gives an added charm to them, while, whatever his theme or your own mood, there is an impetuous, bounding enthusiasm in all that he says,—a strain of exuberant and exulting animal spirits, that carries you whither he wills. A sedate, restrained, dispeptic manner would have been impossible in one writing as he did in all the freshness of inspiration, and in the immediate presence of his objects.

When Audubon had completed his various ornithologies, he projected, with the aid of the Rev. Dr. Bachman, his firm friend, the well-known geologist, a similar work in respect to the quadrupeds. Indeed, he had already, in his previous wanderings, accumulated a large mass of materials, and was only anxious to complete his design. But the approach of age,—he was then nearly seventy,—induced his friends to dissuade him from some of the more toilsome and hazardous expeditions necessary to complete this undertaking. He therefore left a portion of it to Dr. Bachman and to his sons, who inherit much of his talent.

Before this second great undertaking was accomplished the over-wrought constitution had begun to fail, the powers of both mind and body were exhausted—the once brilliant eye could no longer keenly inspect the minute and delicate organs of the smaller quadrupeds or birds, nor could the once firm hand trace aught but trembling lines. We have heard that the last gleam of light stole across his features a few days before his death, when one of his sons held before him, as he sat in his chair, some of his most cherished drawings.

He died on the 27th of January, 1851, gently as a child composes himself to his beautiful sleep. Without show, or the least attempt at parade of any kind, his remains were attended to their resting-place in Trinity Cemetery, adjoining his residence, by his family and a few friends. But in a short space of time the decease of this great, though simple-hearted man was known both throughout our own broad land and Europe.

I cannot but think that his countrymen made too little account of his death. It was perhaps, however, not to be expected that the multitude, who knew nothing of his services, should pay him their tributes of gratitude and respect, but it was to be supposed that our scientific societies and our artist associations would at least propose a monument to one who was so rare an ornament to both. Yet if they were neglectful, there are those who will not be, and who will long cherish his name ; and, in the failure of all human memorial, as it has been elsewhere said, the little wren will whisper it about our homes, the robin and the reed-bird pipe it from the meadows, the ring-dove will coo it from the dewy depths of the woods, and the mountain eagle scream it to the stars.

IRVING

265

I swear to thee, worthy reader, if report belie
not this warrior, I would give all the money in
my pocket to have seen him accoutred cap-a-pie,
in martial array—booted to the middle—sashed
to the chin—collared to the ears—whiskered to
the teeth—crowned with an overshadowing
cocked hat, and girded with a leathern belt ten
inches broad, from which trailed a falchion, of a
length that I dare not mention.

A History of New York.

266

"SUNNYSIDE," The Home of Washington Irving.

IRVING.

BY H. T. TUCKERMAN.*

THE similarity of the landscape in different portions of the country, is often mentioned as a defect in our scenery ; but it has the advantage of constantly affording an epitome of nature and an identity of suggestion favorable to national associations. Without the wild beauty of the Ohio or the luxuriant vegetation of the Mississippi, the Hudson thus preserves a certain verisimilitude in the form of its banks, the windings of its channel, and the hills and trees along its shores, essentially American. The re-

* Written in 1853 for Putnam's *Homes of American Authors.*

flective observer can easily find in these characteristic features, and in the details of the panorama that meets his eye, even during a rapid transit, tokens of all that is peculiar and endeared in the condition and history of his native land ; and it is therefore not less gratifying to his sense of the appropriate than his feeling for the beautiful, that the home of our favorite author should consecrate the scene.

To realize how the Hudson thus identifies itself with national associations, while scanning the details we must bear in mind the general relations of the noble river,—the great metropolis toward which it speeds ; the isle-gemmed bay and adjacent ocean ; and then, reverting to the chain of inland seas with which it is linked, and the junction of its grandest elevations with the vast range of the Alleghanies that intersect the boundless West, recall the intricate network of iron whereby the most distant village that nestles at their feet is connected with its picturesque shores. Thus regarded as a

vital part of a sublime whole, the Hudson
fills the imagination with grandeur while
it fascinates the eye with loveliness.
A few miles from the shores, and in
many instances on the highest ranges of
hills, gleam isolated lakes, fringed with
woods and dotted with small islands,
whence azalea blossoms and feathery
shrubs overhang the water, which is pel-
lucid as crystal, in summer decked with
lilies, in winter affording inexhaustible
quarries of ice, and, at all seasons, the
most romantic haunts for the lover of
nature. Nor is this comprehensive aspect
confined to the river's natural adjuncts.
The immediate localities are equally significant.

On the Jersey shore, which meets
the gaze at the very commencement of
the upward voyage, are visible the grove
where Hamilton fell—the most affecting incident in our political annals ; and
the heights of Weehawken, celebrated by
the muse of Halleck ; soon, on the opposite shore, we descry the evergreen foli-

age of Trinity Church Cemetery, beneath
which lie the remains of that brave explor-
er of the forest and lover of the winged
tribes of the land—Audubon; now rise the
Palisades—nearer landmarks of the bold
stand first taken by the colonists against
British oppression, where Fort Washington was captured by the Hessians in
1776; and whence the enemy's vessels
of war were so adroitly frightened away
by Talbot's fire-ship, and the most perse-
cuted martyrs of the Revolution were
borne to the infamous prison-ship at
Long Island. This wonderful range of
columnar rock, varying in height from
fifty to five hundred feet, and extending
along the river to the distance of twenty
miles, rises perpendicular from the water,
and the channel often runs immediately
at its base. The gray, indented sides of
this natural rampart, its summit tufted
with thickets and a few fishers' huts
nestled at its foot, resemble the ancient
walls of an impregnable fortress; here
and there the traces of a wood-slide mark

its weather-stained face ; and in the stillness of a winter day, when the frozen
water collected in its apertures expands
in the sunshine, from the outer side of
the river may be distinctly heard the
clang of the falling trap-rock dissevered
from the mass.   Opposite are seen the
variegated hills and dales of Westchester
County.   There let us pause, in the neighborhood of our author's residence, to
view the familiar scene amid which he
lives.   Gaze from beneath any of the
porticos that hospitably offer shelter on
the hillsides and at the river's marge,
breathe the pure air, and contemplate the
fresh tints of a June morning.   In this
vicinity the river expands to the width of
two or three miles, forming what is called
Tappan Bay—which, seen from the surrounding eminences, appears like an immense lake ; picturesque undulations
limit the view, meadows covered with
luxuriant grain that waves gracefully in
the breeze, emerald with turf, dark with
copses, or alive with tasselled maize, al-

ternate with clumps of forest-trees or
cheerful orchards. Over this scene of
rural prosperity flit gorgeous clouds
through a firmament of pale azure, and
around it wind roads that seem to lure
the spectator into the beautiful glens of
the neighboring valleys. Nearer to his
eye are patches of woodland, overhanging ravines where rock, foliage, and
stream combine to form a romantic and
sequestered retreat, invaded by no sound
but that of rustling leaf, chirping bird,
humming insect, or snapping chestnut-
burr ; parallel with these delicious nooks
that usually overhang the river, are fields
in the highest state of cultivation surrounding elegant mansions ; but farther
inland stretch pastures where the mullein
grows undisturbed, stone walls and vagrant fences divide fallow acres, the sweet-
briar clambering over their rugged
surface, clumps of elder-bushes or a few
willows clustered about the pond, and
the red cones of the sumac, dead leaves,
brown mushrooms, and downy thistles,

mark one of those neglected yet wildly
rural spots which Crabbe loved to describe. Even here at the sunset hour
we have but to turn towards the river, at
some elevated point, and a scene of inde-
scribable beauty is exhibited. The placid
water is tinted with amber, hues of trans-
cendent brightness glow along the western horizon, fleecy masses of vapor are
illumined with exquisite shades of color;
deep scintillations of rose or purple kin-
dle the edges of the clouds; the zenith
wears a crystalline tone; the vesper star
twinkles with a bright though softened
ray; and the peace of heaven seems to
descend upon the transparent wave and
the balmy air. And if we observe the
immediate scene around one of the humble red-roofed homesteads or superior
dwellings, which are scattered over the
hillsides and valleys of this region, and
call back the vision from its widest to the
most narrow range, the eye is not less gratified, nor the heart less moved, by images
of rustic comfort and beauty. Perhaps a

large tulip-tree, with its broad expanse of
verdure and waving chalices, or a superb
chestnut, plumed with feathery blossoms,
lends its graceful shade, while we follow
the darting swallow, watch the contented
kine, or curiously note the humming-
bird poised, like a fragment of the rain-
bow, over a woodbine wreathed about the
porch, and mark the downy bee clinging
to the mealy stamen of the hollyhock, or
murmuring on the pink globe of the
clover. The odor of the hay-field, the
glancing of countless white sails far below, the flitting of shadows, and the refreshing breeze—all unite to form a picture
of tranquil delight.

Resuming our course, after such an
interlude, we pass the scene of the gal-
lant and unfortunate Andre's capture
and execution. Stony Point, where
another fierce struggle for our liberties
occurred, the site of the fortification
being marked by a lighthouse, the tower-
ing Dunderberg mountain, and that
lofty promontory called Anthony's Nose,

where a sudden turn of the river in a western direction all at once ushers us into the glorious Highlands. The house once occupied by the traitor Arnold is soon forgotten in the thought of Kosciusko, whose monument rises on the precipitous bank at West Point ; and here the wild umbrage that covers Cro'nest recalls Drake's fanciful poem ; and old Fort Putnam, crowning the highest of the majestic hills, seems waiting for the moonbeams to clothe its ruins with enchantment ; Buttermilk Fall glimmers on one side, while the proud summit of the Grand Sachem towers on the other.

Then opens the bay of Newburgh, a town memorable as the spot where the mutinous letters of the Revolution were dated, and where the headquarters and parting scene of Washington and his officers are consecrated to endeared remembrance. Beyond appear the most beautiful domains in the land, where broad ranges of meadow and groups of noble trees, in the highest state of order

and fertility, transport us in fancy to the
rural life of England. The last great feature of this matchless panorama is the
Kaatskill Mountains rising in their misty
shrouds, or, in a clear atmosphere, stretch-
ing away in magnificent proportions,
whence the eye may wander for sixty
miles over a country mapped by prolific
acres, with every shade of verdure—sub-
limated, as it were, by interminable
ranges of mountain, and animated by the
silvery windings of the Hudson, whose
gleaming tide lends brilliancy to the
more dense hues of tree, field, and um-
brageous headland.

The navigable extent of the river, and
the fresh tints of its water, banks, and
sky, are in remarkable contrast with
those celebrated transatlantic streams
endeared to our imagination. To an
American the first view of the Tiber and
the Seine, their turbid waters and flat
shores, occasions peculiar disappointment ; and it is the associations of the
Rhine and Lake Como, and those feat-

ures they derived from art, which chiefly gave them superiority. The mellow light of the past and the charm of an historical name, invest the ruined castles and famed localities of their shores with an enduring interest.

In the spirit of hearty enthusiasm, not less than local attachment, does Irving thank God he was born on the banks of the Hudson ; for it possesses all the elements requisite to inspire the fancy and attach the heart. The blue waving line of its distant hills in the twilight of the early dawn ; the splendid hues of its surrounding foliage in autumn ; the glassy expanse of its broad surface, and the ermine drapery of its majestic promontories in winter; the scene of verdant luxury it presents in summer ; its sheltered nooks, pebbly coves and rocky bluffs ; the echoes of the lofty Highlands, and the balmy hush of evening, when the saffron-tinted water reflects each passing sail, and the cry of the whippoorwill or monotone of the katydid, are the only sounds of life—all utter a mysterious appeal to the senses and imagination.

Washington Irving, although so obviously adapted by natural endowments for the career in which he has acquired such eminence, was educated, like many other men of letters, for the legal profession ; he, however, early abandoned the idea of practice at the bar for the more lucrative vocation of a merchant. His brothers were established in business in the city of New York, and invited him to take an interest in their house, with the understanding that his literary tastes should be gratified by abundant leisure. The unfortunate crisis in mercantile affairs that followed the peace of 1815, involved his family, and threw him upon his own resources for subsistence. To this apparent disaster is owing his subsequent devotion to literature. The strong bias of his own nature, however, had already indicated this destiny ; his inaptitude for affairs, his sensibility to the beautiful, his native humor, and the love he early exhibited for wandering, observing, and indulging in day-dreams, would infallibly have led him to record his fancies and feelings. Indeed, he had already done so with effect, in a series of letters which appeared in a newspaper of which his brother was editor. His tendency to a free, meditative, and adventurous life, was confirmed by a visit to Europe in his early youth.

Born in the city of New York, on the 3d of April, 1783, he pursued his studies, his rambles, and his occasional pen-craft there, until 1804, when ill health made it expedient for him to go abroad. He sailed for Bordeaux, and thence roamed over the most beautiful portions of Southern Europe; visited Switzerland and Holland, sojourned in Paris, and returned home in 1806. During his absence he seriously entertained the idea of becoming a painter; but subsequently resumed his law studies, and was admitted to the bar. Soon after, however, the first number of *Salmagundi* appeared, an era in our literary annals; and in December, 1809, was published *Knickerbocker's History of New York.* He afterwards edited the *Analectic Magazine.* In the autumn of 1814 he joined the military staff of the Governor of New York, as aide-de-camp and secretary, with the title of Colonel. At the close of the war he embarked for Liverpool, with a view of making a second tour in Europe; but the financial troubles intervening, and the remarkable success which had attended his literary enterprises, being an encouragement to pursue a vocation which necessity, not less than taste, now urged him to follow, he embarked in the career of authorship. The papers which were published under the title of *The Sketch-Book*, at once gained him the sympathy and admiration of his contemporaries. They originally appeared in New York, but attracted immediate attention in England, and were republished there in 1820. After residing there five years, Mr. Irving again visited

Paris, and returned to bring out *Brace-bridge Hall* in London, in May, 1822. The next winter he passed in Dresden, and in the following spring put *Tales of a Traveller* to press. He soon after went to Madrid and wrote the *Life of Colum-bus*, which appeared in 1828. In the spring of that year he visited the South of Spain, and the result was the *Chroni-cles of the Conquest of Granada*, which was published in 1829. The same year he revisited that region, and collected the materials for his *Alhambra*. He was soon after appointed Secretary of Lega-tion to the American Embassy in London, which office he held until the return of Mr. McLane in 1831.

While in England he received one of the fifty-guinea gold medals, pro-vided by George IV., for eminence in historical composition, and the degree of LL.D. from the University of Oxford. His return to New York in 1832 was greeted by a festival, at which were gathered his surviving friends and all the illustrious men of his native metropolis. The following summer he accompanied one of the Commissioners for removing the Indian tribes west of the Mississippi. The fruit of this excursion was his graphic *Tour on the Prairies*. Soon after appeared *Abbotsford and Newstead Abbey*, and *Legends of the Conquest of Spain*. In 1836 he published *Astoria*, and in 1837 *The Adventures of Captain Bonneville*. In 1839 he contributed several papers to the *Knickerbocker's Magazine*. Early in 1842 he was appointed Minister to Spain. On his return to this country in 1846, he began a publication of a revised edition of his works, to the list of which he has since added a *Life of Goldsmith* and *Mahomet and his Successors;* and he is now engaged upon a Life of Washington.

This outline should be filled by the reader's imagination with the accessories and the coloring incident to so varied, honorable and congenial a life. In all his wanderings, his eye was busied with the scenes of nature, and cognizant of their every feature, his memory brooded over the traditions of the past, and his heart caught and reflected every phase of humanity. With the feelings of a poet and the habitudes of an artist, he thus wandered over the rural districts of merry England, the melancholy hills of romantic Spain, and the exuberant wilderness of his native land, gathering up their most picturesque aspects, and their most affecting legends, and transferring them, with the pure and vivid colors of his genial expression, into permanent memorials. Every quaint outline, every mellow tint, the aerial prospective that leads the sight into the mazes of antiquity, the amusing still-life or characteristic human attributes,—all that excites wonder, sympathy, and merriment, he thus recognized and preserved ; and shed over all the sunny atmosphere of a kindly heart and the freshness of a natural zest, and the attraction of a modest character, —a combination which has been happily characterized by Lowell in the *Fable for Critics:*

What ! Irving ? Thrice welcome, warm heart
    and fine brain,
  You bring back the happiest spirit from Spain,
  And the gravest sweet humor, that ever were
      there
  Since Cervantes met death in his gentle de-
      spair ;
  Nay, don't be embarrassed, nor look so be-
      seeching,
  I shan't run directly against my own preach-
      ing,
  And having just laughed at their Raphaels and
      Dantes,
  Go to setting you up beside matchless Cer-
      vantes ;
  But allow me to speak what I honestly feel,
  To a true poet-heart add the fun of Dick Steele,
  Throw in all of Addison, minus the chill,
  With the whole of that partnership's stock and
      good-will,
  Mix well, and while stirring, hum o'er as a
      spell,
  The 'fine old English Gentleman,' simmer it
      well,
  Sweeten just to your own private liking, then
      strain,
  That only the finest and clearest remain.
  Let it stand out of doors till a soul it receives
  From the warm lazy sun loitering down
      through green leaves,
  And you 'll find a choice nature not wholly
      deserving
  A name either English or Yankee—just Ir-
      ving.

Irving

The eminent success which has attended the late republication of Irving's
works, teaches a lesson that we hope will
not be lost on the cultivators of literature. It proves a truth which all men of
enlightened taste intuitively feel, but
which is constantly forgotten by perverse
aspirants for literary fame ; and that is
—the permanent value of a direct, simple
and natural style. It is not only the
genial philosophy, the humane spirit, the
humor and pathos of Irving, which en-
dear his writings and secure for them
an habitual interest, but it is the refreshment afforded by a recurrence to the
unalloyed, unaffected, clear, and flowing
style in which he invariably expresses
himself.

The place which our author holds in
national affection can never be super-
seded. His name is indissolubly associated with the dawn of our recognized
literary culture. We have always regarded his popularity in England as one
of the most charming traits of his reputa-

tion, and that, too, for the very reasons
which narrow critics once assigned as de-
rogatory to his national spirit.   His treatment of English subjects ; the felicitous
manner in which he revealed the life of
our ancestral land to us, her prosperous
offspring, mingled as it was with vivid
pictures of our own scenery, touched a
cord in the heart which responds to all
that is generous in sympathy and noble
in association.   If we regard Irving with
national pride and affection, it is partly
on account of his cosmopolitan tone of
mind—a quality, among others, in which
he greatly resembles Goldsmith.   It is,
indeed, worthy of a true American writer
that, with his own country and a particular region thereof as a nucleus of his
sentiment, he can see and feel the characteristic and the beautiful, not only in
old England, but in romantic Spain ;
that the phlegmatic Dutchman and the
mercurial southern European find an
equal place in his comprehensive glance.
To range from the local wit of *Salma-*

---

gundi to the grand and serious historical enterprise which achieved a classic *Life of Columbus*, and from the simple grief embalmed in the "Widow's Son" to the observant humor of "The Stout Gentleman," bespeaks not only an artist of exquisite and versatile skill, but a man of the most liberal heart and catholic taste.

Reputations, in their degree and kind, are as legitimate subjects of taste as less abstract things,—and in that of Washington Irving there is a completeness and unity seldom realized. It accords, in its unchallenged purity, with the harmonious character of the author and the serene attractions of his home. By temperament and cast of mind he was ordained to be a gentle minister at the altar of literature, an interpreter of the latent music of nature and the redeeming affections of humanity ; and, with a consistency not less dictated by good sense than true feeling, he has distinctively adhered to the sphere he was especially gifted to

adorn. Since his advent as a writer, an
intense style has come into vogue ; glowing rhetoric, bold verbal tactics, and a
more powerful exercise of thought characterize many of the popular authors of the
day. But in literature as in life, there
are various provinces both of utility and
taste ; and in this country and age a
conservative tone, a reliance on the
kindly emotions, and the refined percep-
tions, are qualities eminently desirable.
Therefore as we look forth upon the calm
and picturesque landscape that environs
him, we are content that no fierce po-
lemic, visionary philanthropist, or morbid sentimentalist has thus linked his
name with the tranquil beauties of the
scene ; but that it is the home of an author who, with graceful diction and an
affectionate heart, celebrates the scenic
charms of the outward world and the
harmless eccentricities and natural sentiment of the race. The true bias of Irving's genius is artistic. The lights and
shadows of English life, the legendary

a season for the lifting of the heel as
well as the heart; labor came dancing
in the train of abundance and frolic
prevailed throughout the land. Hoppe dell,

FACSIMILE OF MANUSCRIPT OF IRVING'S "KNICKERBOCKER NEW YORK."

were joyous gatherings of the two
sexes to dance and make merry.
Now were instituted "quilting bees"
and "husking bees" and other rural as-
semblages where, under the inspiring
influence of the fiddle toil was lightened by gaiety and followed up by the
dance. "Raising bees" also were
frequent, where houses sprang up at
the waggery of the fiddlestick, as the
walls of Thebes sprang up of yore
to the sound of the lyre of Amphion

Jolly autumn, which pours its treasures
over hill and dale was, in those days
a season for the lifting of the heel as
well as the heart; labor came dancing
in the train of abundance and foolie
frowned throughout the land. Hoppe czssh

romance of Spain, the novelties of a tour on the Prairies of the West, and of adventures in the Rocky Mountains, the poetic beauty of the Alhambra, the memories of Abbotsford and Newstead Abbey, the quaint and comfortable philosophy of the Dutch colonists, and the scenery of the Hudson, are themes upon which he expatiates with the grace and zest of a master. His affinity of style with the classic British essayists, served not only as an invaluable precedent in view of the crude mode of expression prevalent half a century ago among us, but also proved a bond in letters between our own country and England, by recalling the identity of language and domestic life, at a time when great asperity of feeling divided the two countries.

The circumstances of our daily life and the impulse of our national destiny, amply insure the circulation of progressive and practical ideas ; but there is little in either to sustain a wholesome attachment to the past, or inspire disinterested feelings and imaginative recreation. Accordingly we rejoice that our literary pioneer is not only an artist of the beautiful, but one whose pencil is dipped in the mellow tints of legendary lore, who infuses the element of repose and the sportiveness of fancy into his creations, and thus yields genuine refreshment and a needed lesson to the fevered minds of his countrymen. Of all his immortal pictures, however, the most precious to his countrymen is that which contains the house of old Baltus Van Tassel, especially since it has been refitted and ornamented by Geoffrey Crayon ; and pleasant as it is to their imagination as Wolfert's Roost, it is far more dear to their hearts as Sunnyside.

And the legends which he has so gracefully woven around every striking point in the scene, readily assimilate with its character, whether they breathe grotesque humor, harmless superstition, or pensive sentiment. We smile habitually and with the same zest, at the idea of the

Trumpeter's rubicund proboscis, the valiant defence of Bearn Island, and the figure which the pedagogue cuts on the dorsal ridge of old Gunpowder; and, inhaling the magnetic atmosphere of Sleepy Hollow, we easily give credit to the apparition of the Headless Horseman, and have no desire to repudiate the frisking imps of the Duyvel's Dans Kamer. The buxom charms of Katrina Van Tassel, and the substantial comforts of her paternal farmhouse, are as tempting to us as they once were to the unfortunate Ichabod and the successful Brom Bones.

The mansion of this prosperous and valiant family, so often celebrated in his writings, is the residence of Washington Irving. It is approached by a sequestered road, which enhances the effect of its natural beauty. A more tranquil and protected abode, nestled in the lap of nature, never captivated a poet's eye. Rising from the bank of the river, which a strip of woodland alone intercepts, it

unites every rural charm to the most
complete seclusion. From this interesting domain is visible the broad surface
of the Tappan Zee; the grounds slope to
the water's edge, and are bordered by
wooded ravines; a clear brook ripples
near, and several neat paths lead to shadowy walks or fine points of river scenery.
The house itself is a graceful combination
of the English cottage and the Dutch
farmhouse. The crow-stepped gables,
the tiles in the hall, and the weather-
cocks, partake of the latter character;
while the white walls gleaming through
the trees, the smooth and verdant turf,
and the mantling vines of ivy and clambering roses, suggest the former. Indeed, in this delightful homestead are
tokens of all that is most characteristic
of its owner. The simplicity and rustic
grace of the abode indicate an unper-
verted taste,—its secluded position a love
of veiled pictures of English country-life;
the weathercock that used to veer about
on the Stadthouse of Amsterdam, is a

symbol of the fatherland ; while the one that adorned the grand dwellings in Albany before the Revolution, is a significant memorial of the old Dutch colonists ; and they are thus both associated with the fragrant memory of that famous and unique historian, Diedrich Knickerbocker. The quaint and the beautiful are thus blended, and the effect of the whole is singularly harmonious. From the quietude of this retreat are obtainable the most extensive prospects ; and while its sheltered position breathes the very air of domestic repose, the scenery it commands is eloquent of broad and generous sympathies.

Not less rare than beautiful is the lot of the author to whom it is permitted to gather up the memorials of his fame and witness their permanent recognition,— the first partial favor of his contemporaries renewed by the mature appreciation of another generation ; and equally gratifying is the coincidence of such a noble satisfaction with a return to the cher-

ished and picturesque haunts of childhood and youth. It is a phase of life
scarcely less delightful to contemplate
than to enjoy; and we agree with a native artist who declares that in his many
trips up and down the Hudson, he never
passed Sunnyside without a thrill of
pleasure. Nor, if thus interesting even
as an object in the landscape, is it difficult to imagine what moral attractions it
possesses to the kindred and friends who
there habitually enjoy such genial companionship and frank hospitality. To
this favored spot, around which his
fondest reminiscences hovered during a
long absence, Mr. Irving returned a few
years since, crowned with the purest literary renown, and as much attached to
his native scenery as when he wandered
there in the holiday reveries of boyhood.
And here, in the midst of a landscape his
pen has made attractive in both hemispheres, and of friends whose love surpasses the highest need of fame, he lives
in daily view of scenes thrice endeared—

by taste, association, and habit—the old
locust that blossoms on the green bank
in spring, the brook that sparkles along
the grass, the peaked turret and vine-
covered wall of that modest yet traditional dwelling, the favorite valley
watered by the romantic Pocantico, and,
above all, the glorious river of his heart.

We are strongly tempted to record
some of the charming anecdotes which
fall from his lips in the hour of genial
companionship; to revert to the details
of his personal career; the remarkable
coincidences by which he became a spectator of some of the most noted occur-
rences of the last half-century ; — his
personal intercourse with the gifted and
renowned of both hemispheres ; the fond
admiration manifested by his countrymen
in making his name familiar as a household word, on their ships and steamers,
their schools, hotels, and townships ; the
beautiful features of his domestic life ; the
affectionate reverence with which he is
regarded by his relatives and his immedi-

ate friends and neighbors ; the refined yet joyous tone of his truly "Sunnyside" hospitalities, so charmingly enlivened by his humorous and historical reminiscences. But two considerations warn us from these seductive topics—the one a cherished hope that the reminiscences thus briefly alluded to may yet be gathered up in his own hand ; the other our knowledge of his delicacy of feeling and sensitive habit in regard to personalities. In a letter to the editor of the *Knickerbocker Magazine*, Mr. Irving, under the character of Geoffrey Crayon, gives an account of his purchase of the Van Tassel estate, now called "Sunnyside," and a characteristic description of the neighborhood, which abounds in some of the happiest touches of his style. This letter was a commencement of a series of articles published in the *Knickerbocker*, which, excepting his *Life of Goldsmith*, are the last of his published writings.

LONGFELLOW.

This is the place.   Stand still, my steed,
　Let me review the scene ;
And summon from the shadowy Past
　The forms that once have been.
A Gleam of Sunshine.

HOME OF LONGFELLOW, Cambridge, Mass.

LONGFELLOW.

BY GEORGE WILLIAM CURTIS.*

ONE calm afternoon in the summer of 1837, a young man passed down the elm-shaded walk that separated the old Craigie House in Cambridge from the highroad. Reaching the door, he paused to observe the huge, old-fashioned brass knocker and the quaint handle,—relics, evidently, of an epoch of colonial state. To his mind, however, the house and these signs of its age, were not interesting from the romance of antiquity alone, but from their association with the early days of

* Written in 1853 for Putnam's *Homes of American Authors.*

our revolution, when General Washington, after the battle of Bunker Hill, had his headquarters in the mansion. Had his hand, perhaps, lifted this same latch, lingering as he clasped it in the whirl of a myriad emotions? Had he, too, paused in the calm summer afternoon, and watched the silver gleam of the broad river in the meadows—the dreamy blue of the Milton hills beyond? And had the tranquillity of that landscape penetrated his heart with "the sleep that is among the hills," and whose fairest dream to him was a hope now realized in the peaceful prosperity of his country?

At least the young man knew that if the details of the mansion had been somewhat altered, so that he could not be perfectly sure of touching what Washington touched, yet he saw what Washington saw—the same placid meadow-lands, the same undulating horizon, the same calm stream. And it is thus that an old house of distinct association, asserts its claim and secures its influence. It is a nucleus of interest,—a heart of romance, from which pulse a thousand reveries enchanting the summer hours. For although every old country mansion is invested with a nameless charm, from that antiquity which imagination is forever crowding with the pageant of a stately and beautiful life, yet if there be some clearly outlined story, even a historic scene peculiar to it, then around that, as the bold and picturesque foreground, all the imagery of youth, and love, and beauty, in a thousand-fold variety of development, is grouped, and every room has its poetic passage, every window its haunting face, every garden-path its floating and fading form of a quite imperishable beauty.

So the young man passed not unaccompanied down the elm-shaded path, and the air and the scene were affluent of radiant phantoms. Imaginary ladies, of a state and dignity only possible in the era of periwigs, advanced in all the solemnity of mob-caps to welcome the stranger. Grave old courtiers, beruffled, bewigged, sworded, and laced, trod inaudibly, with gracious bow, the spacious walk; and comely maidens, resident in mortal memory now only as shrivelled and tawny duennas, glanced modest looks, and wondered what new charm had risen that morning upon the somewhat dull horizon of their life. These, arrayed in the richness of a poet's fancy, advanced to welcome him. For well they knew whatever of peculiar interest adorned their house would blossom into permanent forms of beauty in the light of genius. They advanced to meet, as the inhabitants of foreign and strange towns approach, with supplication and submission, the leader in whose eyes flames victory, sure that he would do for them more than they could do for themselves.

But when the brazen clang of the huge knocker had ceased resounding, the great door slowly opened, and no phantom serving-man, but a veritable flesh and blood retainer of the hostess of the mansion invited the visitor to enter. He inquired for Mrs. Craigie. In answer, the door of a little parlor was thrown open, and the young man beheld a tall, erect figure, majestically crowned with a turban, beneath which burned a pair of keen gray eyes. A commanding gravity of deportment, harmonious with the gentle-woman's age, and with the ancestral respectability of the mansion, assured profound respect ; while, at a glance, it was clear to see that combination of reduced dignity condescending to a lower estate, and that pride of essential superiority to circumstances, which is traditional among women in the situation of the turbaned lady. There was kindliness mellowing the severity of her reply to her visitor's inquiry if there was a room vacant in the house.

"I lodge students no longer," she responded gravely, possibly not without regret—as she contemplated the applicant—that she had vowed so stern a resolution.

"But I am not a student," answered the stranger; "I am a professor in the University."

"A professor?" said she inquiringly, as if her mind failed to conceive a professor without a clerical sobriety of apparel, a white cravat, or at least spectacles.

"Professor Longfellow," continued the guest, introducing himself.

"Ah! that is different," said the old lady, her features slightly relaxing, as if professors were, *ex-officio*, innocuous, and she need no longer barricade herself behind a stern gravity of demeanor. "I will show you what there is."

Thereupon she preceded the Professor up the stairs, and gaining the upper hall, paused at each door, opened it, permitted him to perceive its delightful fitness for his purpose,—kindled expectation to the utmost—then quietly closed the door again, observing: "You cannot have that." It was most Barmecide hospitality. The professorial eyes glanced restlessly around the fine old-fashioned points of the mansion, marked the wooden carvings, the air of opulent respectability in the past, which corresponds in New England to the impression of ancient nobility in old England, and wondered in which of these pleasant fields of suggestive association he was to be allowed to pitch his tent. The turbaned hostess at length opened the door of the southeast corner room in the second story, and, while the guest looked wistfully in and awaited the customary, " You cannot have that," he was agreeably surprised by a variation of the strain to the effect that he might occupy it.

The room was upon the front of the house, and looked over the meadows to the river. It had an atmosphere of fascinating repose, in which the young man was at once domesticated, as in an old home. The elms of the avenue shaded his windows, and as he glanced from them, the summer lay asleep upon the landscape in the windless day.

" This," said the old lady, with a slight sadness in her voice, as if speaking of times forever past and to which she herself properly belonged,—"this was General Washington's chamber."

A light more pensive played over the landscape, in the Poet's eyes, as he heard her words. He knew that such a presence had consecrated the house, and peculiarly that room. He felt that whoever fills the places once occupied by the great and good, is himself held to greatness and goodness by a sympathy and necessity sweet as mysterious. Forever after, his imagination is a more lordly picture-gallery than that of ancestral halls. Through that gallery he wanders, strong in his humility and resolve, valiant as the last scion of noble Norman races, devoting himself, as of old knights were devoted, by earnest midnight meditation and holy vows, to

> Act,—act in the living Present !
> Heart within and God o'erhead !

The stately hostess retired, and the next day the new lodger took possession of his room. He lived entirely apart from the old lady, although under the same roof. Her manner of life was quiet and unobtrusive. The silence of the ancient mansion, which to its new resident was truly "the still air of delightful studies," was not disturbed by the shrill cackle of a country household. In the morning, after he had settled himself to the day's occupation, the scholar heard the faint and measured tread of the old lady as she descended to breakfast, her silken gown rustling along the hall as if the shadowy brocade of some elder dame departed, who failed to discover in the ghostly stillness of the well-known passage, that she had wandered from her sphere. Then, after due interval, if, upon his way to the day's collegiate duties, the professor entered the hostess's little parlor to offer her good morning, he found her seated by the open window, through which stole the sweet New England air, lifting the few gray locks that straggled from the turban, as tenderly as Greek winds played with Helen's curls. Upon her lap lay an open volume of Voltaire, possibly, for the catholicity of the old lady's mind entertained whatever was vigorous and free,—and from the brilliant wit of the Frenchman, and his icy precision of thought and statement, she turned to the warm day that flooded the meadows with summer, and which in the high tree-tops above her head sang in breezy, fitful cadences of a beauty that no denizen of the summer shall ever see, and a song sweeter than he shall ever hear. It was because she had heard and felt this breath of nature that the matron in her quaint old age could enjoy the page of the Frenchman, even as in her youth she could have admired the delicacy of his point-lace ruffles, nor have less enjoyed, by reason of that admiration, the green garden-walk of Ferney, in which she might have seen them.

Or at times, as the scholar studied, he heard footsteps upon the walk, and the old knocker clanged the arrival of guests,

who passed into the parlor, and, as the
door opened and closed, he could hear,
far away and confused, the sounds of
stately conversation, until there was a
prolonged and louder noise, a bustle, the
jar of the heavy door closing, the dying
echo of footsteps,—and then the deep and
ghostly silence again closed around the
small event as the sea ripples into calm
over a sinking stone.   Or more dreamily
still, as at twilight the poet sat musing
in his darkening room—hearing the
" footsteps of angels " sounding, melodious and low, through all the other
" voices of the night,"—he seemed to
catch snatches of mournful music thrilling the deep silence with sorrow, and,
listening more intently, he heard distinctly the harpsichord in the old lady's
parlor, and knew that she was sitting,
turbaned and wrinkled, where she had
sat in the glowing triumph of youth, and
with wandering fingers was drawing in
feeble and uncertain cadence from the
keys, tunes she had once dashed from

them in all the fulness of harmony. Or when, the summer following the poet's arrival, the blight of canker-worms fell upon the stately old trees before the house, and struck them mortally, so that they gradually wasted and withered away, —if then the young man entered her parlor and finding her by the open window, saw that the worms were crawling over her dress and hanging from her white turban, and asked her if they were not disagreeable and if she would do nothing to destroy them, she raised her eyes from another book than Voltaire's, and said to him gravely: "Why, sir, they are our fellow-worms, and have as good a right to live as we." And as the poet returned to his chamber, musing more than ever upon the Saturn Time that so remorselessly consumes his own children, and picturing the gay youth of the grave old hostess, he could not but pause, leaning upon the heavy balusters of the stairs and remember the tradition of the house, that once, as an old hostess, like his own, lay waiting for death in her chamber, she sent for her young guest, like himself, to come and take last leave of her, and as he entered her room, and advancing to her bedside, saw her lying stretched at length and clutching the clothes around her neck, so that only her sharply featured and shrunken face was visible,— the fading eye opened upon him for a moment and he heard from the withered lips this stern whisper of farewell: "Young man, never marry, for beauty comes to this!"

The lines of the Poet had fallen in pleasant places. With the old house and its hostess, and its many known and unknown associations, there was no lack of material for thought and speculation. A country house in New England which is not only old, but by the character of its structure and its coherent history, suggests a life of more interest and dignity than that of a simple countryman "whose only aim was to increase his store," is interesting in the degree of its rarity.

The traveller upon the highroad before the Craigie House, even if he knew nothing of its story, would be struck by its quaint dignity and respectability, and make a legend, if he could not find one already made. If, however, his lot had been cast in Cambridge, and he had been able to secure a room in the mansion, he would not rest until he had explored the traditions of its origin and occupancy, and had given his fancy moulds in which to run its images. He would have found in the churchyard of Cambridge a freestone tablet supported by five pillars, upon which, with the name, Col. John Vassal, died in 1747, are sculptured the words, Vas-sol, and the emblems, a goblet and sun. Whether this device was a proud assertion of the fact, that the fortunes of the family should be always as

A beaker full of the warm South,

happily no historian records; for the beaker has long since been drained to the dregs, and of the stately family nothing survived in the early part of the poet's residence in the house, but an old black man who had been born, a slave, in the mansion during the last days of the Vassals, and who occasionally returned to visit his earliest haunts, like an Indian the hunting-grounds of his extinct tribe.

This Col. John Vassal is supposed to have built the house towards the close of the first half of the last century. Upon an iron in the back of one of the chimneys, there is the date, 1759, which probably commemorates no more than the fact of its own insertion at that period, inasmuch as the builder of the house would hardly commit the authentic witness of its erection to the mercies of smoke and soot. History capitulates before the exact date of the building of the Craigie House, as completely as before that of the foundation of Thebes. But the house was evidently generously built, and Col. John Vassal having lived there in generous style, died, and lies under the free-stone tablet. His son John fell upon revolutionary times, and was a royalist. The observer of the house will not be surprised at the fact. That the occupant of such a mansion should, in colonial troubles, side with the government, was as natural as the fealty of a Douglas or a Howard to the king.

The house, however, passed from his hands, and was purchased by the provincial government at the beginning of serious work with the mother country. After the battle of Bunker Hill, it was allotted to George Washington as his headquarters. It was entirely unfurnished, but the charity of neighbors filled it with necessary furniture. The southeastern room upon the lower floor, at the right of the front door, and now occupied as a study by Mr. Longfellow, was devoted to the same purpose by Washington. The room over it, as Madame Craigie has already informed us, was his chamber. The room upon the lower floor, in the rear of the study, which was afterwards enlarged and is now the Poet's library, was occupied by the aides-de-camp of the commander-in-chief. And the southwest room, upon the lower floor, was Mrs. Washington's drawing room. The rich old wood carving in this apartment is still remarkable, still certifies the frequent presence of fine society. For, although during the year in which Washington occupied the mansion, there could have been as little desire as means for gay festivity ; yet Washington and his leading associates were all gentlemen — men who would have graced the elegance of a court with the same dignity that made the plainness of a republic admirable. Many of Washington's published letters are dated from this house. And could the walls whisper, we should hear more and better things of him than could ever be recorded. In his chamber are still the gay-painted tiles peculiar to fine houses of the period ; and upon their quaint and grotesque images the glancing eyes of the Poet's children now wonderingly linger, where the sad and doubtful ones of Washington must have often fallen as he meditated the darkness of the future.

Many of these peculiarities and memories of the mansion appear in the Poet's verses. In the opening of the poem *To a Child* the tiles are painted anew.

> The lady with the gay macaw,
> The dancing girl, the brave Bashaw
>   With bearded lip and chin ;
> And, leaning idly o'er his gate,
> Beneath the imperial fan of state,
>   The Chinese mandarin.

The next figure that distinctly appears in the old house is that of Thomas Tracy, a personage of whom the household traditions are extremely fond. He was a rich man, in the fabulous style of the East ; such a nabob as Oriental imaginations can everywhere easily conjure, while practical experience wonders that they are so rare. He carried himself with a rare lavishness. Servants drank costly wines from carved pitchers in the incredible days of Thomas Tracy ; and in his stately mansion, a hundred guests sat down to banquets, and pledged their hosts in draughts whose remembrance keeps his name sweet, as royal bodies were preserved in wine and spices. In the early days of national disorder, he sent out privateers to scour the seas and bleed Spanish galleons of their sunniest juices, and reap golden harvests of fruits and spices, of silks and satins, from East and West Indian ships, that the bountiful table of Vassal House might not fail, nor the carousing days of Thomas Tracy become credible. But these "spacious times" of the large-hearted and large-handed gentleman suddenly ended. The wealthy man failed; no more hundred guests appeared at banquets; no more privateers sailed into Boston Bay, reeking with riches from every zone; Spain, the Brazils, the Indies, no more rolled their golden sands into the pockets of Thomas Tracy; servants, costly wines, carved pitchers, all began to glimmer and go, and finally Thomas Tracy and

his incredible days vanished as entirely
as the gorgeous pavilions with which the
sun in setting piles the summer west.

After this illuminated chapter in the
history of the house, Captain Joseph Lee,
a brother of Madame Tracy, appears in
the annals, but does not seem to have
illustrated them by any special gifts or
graces. Tradition remains silent, pining
for Thomas Tracy, until it lifts its head
upon the entry into the house of Andrew
Craigie, Apothecary-General to the Northern Provincial Army, who amassed a fortune in that office, which, like his great
predecessor, he presently lost ; but not
until he had built a bridge over the
Charles River, connecting Cambridge
with Boston, which is still known by his
name. Andrew Craigie did much for the
house, even enlarging it to its present
form ; but tradition is hard upon him. It
declares that he was a huge man, heavy
and dull ; and evidently looks upon his
career as the high lyric of Thomas
Tracy's, muddled into tough prose. In

the best and most prosperous days of Andrew Craigie, the estate comprised two hundred acres. Upon the site of the present observatory, not far from the mansion, stood a summer-house, but whether of any rare architectural device, whether, in fact, any orphic genius of those days made a summer house, which, like that of Mr. Emerson's, only "lacked scientific arrangement" to be quite perfect, does not appear. Like the apothecary to the Northern army, the summer-house is gone, as likewise an aqueduct that brought water a quarter of a mile. Tradition, so enamoured of Tracy is generous enough to mention a dinner-party given by Andrew Craigie every Saturday, and on one occasion points out peruked and powdered Talleyrand among the guests. This betrays the presence in the house of the best society then to be had. But the prosperous Craigie could not avoid the fate of his opulent predecessor, who also gave banquets. Things rushed on too rapidly for him. The bridge, aqueduct, and summer-house, two hundred acres and an enlarged house, were too much for the fortune acquired in dealing medicaments to the Northern army. The "spacious times" of Andrew Craigie also came to an end. A visitor walked with him through his large and handsome rooms, and struck with admiration, exclaimed:

"Mr. Craigie, I should think you could lose yourself in all this spaciousness."

"Mr. ——" (tradition has forgotten the name), said the hospitable and ruined host, "I *have* lost myself in it,"—and we do not find him again.

After his disappearance Mrs. Craigie, bravely swallowing the risings of pride, and still revealing in her character and demeanor the worthy mistress of a noble mansion, let rooms. Edward Everett resided here just after his marriage, and while still professor in the college of which he was afterward President. Willard Phillips, Jared Sparks, now the head of the University, and Joseph E. Worces-

Send Proof to
Henry W. Longfellow.
Cambridge .

FACSIMILE OF MANUSCRIPT OF LONGFELLOW'S "THE FIFTH PSALM."

ter, the Lexicographer, have all resided here, sometimes sharing the house with Mrs. Craigie, and, in the case of Mr. Worcester, occupying it jointly with Mr. Longfellow when the grave old lady removed her stately turban for the last time.

The Craigie House is now the Poet's, and has again acquired a distinctive interest in history. It was in Portland, Maine, in the year 1807, and in an old square wooden house upon the edge of the sea, that Longfellow was born. The old house stood upon the outskirts of the town, separated only by a street from the water. In the lower story there is now a shop,—a bookseller's doubtless, muses imagination,—so that the same house which gave a singer to the world may offer to the world his songs to justify its pride in him. He graduated at Brunswick with Hawthorne, whom then the Poet knew only as a shy youth in a bright-buttoned coat, flitting across the college grounds. During his college days he wooed the muses, as all students woo ; and in the *United States Library Gazette*, then published in Boston, the world learned how his suit prospered. In 1826 Longfellow first visited Europe. He loitered through France, Spain, Italy, Germany, Holland, and England, and returned to America in 1829. Appointed Professor in his Alma Mater, he devoted himself to the scholar's life, poring long and earnestly over the literature of lands which he knew so well and truly that their literature lived for him and was not a hard hieroglyph only. During these quiet professorial years he contributed articles to the *North American Review*, a proceeding not unprecedented among New England scholars, and in which Emerson, the Everetts, and all the more illustrious of the literary men of the North, have been participants. The forms of foreign travel gradually grouped themselves in his mind. Vivid pictures of European experience, such as illuminate the memory of every young and romantic traveller, constantly flashed along his way, and he began to retrace them in words, that others might know, according to the German proverb, that "behind the mountains there are men also."

In this way commenced the publication of *Outre Mer, or Sketches from Beyond the Sea*, a work of foreign reminiscences, tales and reveries of the life peculiar to Europe. It was published, originally, in numbers, by Samuel Colman, a townsman of the author's. Like the *Sketch-Book*, it was issued whenever a number was prepared, but unlike the author of the *Sketch-Book*, the Professor could not write as his motto, " I have no wife nor children, good or bad, to provide for " ; for in the midst of the quiet professorial days, still a very young man, the Poet was married,—a fleeting joy ending by the death of his wife in Rotterdam in 1835. In Brunswick, also, and at this time, he made the translation of the ode upon *Coplas de Manrique*, by his son Don Jozé Manrique, a rich, mournfully-

rolling Spanish poem. The earlier verses
of the young man had made their mark.
In school reading-books, and in volumes
of elegant extracts, and preserved in
many a daintily ribboned manuscript,
the *April Day*, *Woods in Winter*,
*Hymn of the Moravian Nuns at Bethle-
hem*, *Burial of the Minnisink*, and
others, were readily found. As yet the
Poet was guiltless of a volume, but his
name was known, and upon the credit of
a few fugitive pieces he was mentioned
first after the monopolizing masters of
American verse.

In the year 1835 he received the ap-
pointment of Professor in Harvard College, Cambridge, which he accepted, but
sailed for Europe again in the course of
the year. Upon leaving he committed
the publication of *Outre Mer* to the
Harpers in New York, who issued the
entire work in two volumes. The second
European visit was confined to the north
of Europe, Denmark, England, Sweden,
Germany, a long pause in Holland, and

Paris. In the autumn of 1836 he returned, and in December of the same year removed to Cambridge to reside. Here, again, the *North American Review* figures a little in the literary life of the Poet. He wrote several articles for it during the leisure of his engagements as Professor of Modern Literature, and, at length, as we have seen, one calm afternoon in the summer of 1837, Longfellow first took lodgings in the Craigie House, with which the maturity and extent of his reputation was to be so closely associated.

Some wan ghost of Thomas Tracy, lordly with lace and gracious in perfumed pomp, surely the Poet saw advancing, holding in his hand some one of these antique carved pitchers brimmed with that costly wine, and exhorting him to drain potent draughts, that not by him should the fame of the incredible days be tarnished, but that, as when a hundred guests sat at the banquet, and a score of full-freighted ships arrived for Thomas Tracy, the traveller should say,

A purple light shines over all,
It beams from the luck of Edenhall.

The vow was pledged, and now under the few elms that remain of those which the fellow-worms of Mrs. Craigie blighted, the ghost of Thomas Tracy walks appeased.

In his still southeastern upper chamber, in which Washington had also slept, the Poet wrote *Hyperion* in the years 1838-9. It is truly a romance, a beaker of the wine of youth, and was instantly received as such by the public. That public was, and must always be, of the young. No book had appeared which so admirably expressed the romantic experience of every poetic young mind in Europe, and an experience which will be constantly renewed. Probably no American book had ever so passionate a popularity as *Hyperion*. It was published in the summer of 1839 by Colman, who had then removed to New York, but at the time of publication he failed, and it was undertaken by John Owen, the University publisher in Cambridge. It is a singular tribute to the integrity of the work, and a marked illustration of the peculiarity of American development, that Horace Greeley, famous as a political journalist, and intimately associated with every kind of positive and practical movement, was among the very earliest of the warmest lovers of *Hyperion*. It shows our national eclecticism of sentiment and sense, which is constantly betraying itself in a thousand and other ways.

Here, too, in the southeast chamber, were written the *Voices of the Night*, published in 1840. Some of the more noted, such as the *Psalm of Life*, had already appeared in the *Knickerbocker Magazine*. Strangely enough as a fact in American literary history, the fame of the romance was even surpassed, and one of the most popular books of the day was *Longfellow's Poems*. They were read everywhere by every one, and were republished and have continued to be republished in England and in various other countries. The secret of his popularity as a poet is probably that of all similar popularity, namely, the fact that his poetry expresses a universal sentiment in the simplest and most melodious manner. Each of his most noted poems is the song of a feeling common to every mind in moods into which every mind is liable to fall. Thus *A Psalm of Life, Footsteps of Angels, To the River Charles, Excelsior, The Bridge, A Gleam of Sunshine, The Day is Done, The Old Clock on the Stairs, The Arrow and the Song, The Fire of Driftwood, Twilight, The Open Window*, are all most adequate and inexpressibly delicate renderings of quite universal emotions. There is a humanity in them which is irresistible in the fit measures to which they are wedded. If some elegiac poets have strung rosaries of tears, there is a weakness of woe in their verses which repels; but the quiet, pensive thought,—the twilight of the mind, in which the little facts of life are saddened in view of their relation to the eternal laws, time and change,—this is the meditation and mourning of every manly heart ; and this is the alluring and permanent charm of Longfellow's poetry.

In 1842 the Ballads and other Poems were published, and in the same year the Poet sailed again for Europe. He passed the summer upon the Rhine, residing some time at Boppart, where he saw much of the ardent young German poet Freiligrath. He returned after a few months, composing the poems on slavery during the homeward passage. Upon landing, he found the world drunken with the grace of Fanny Ellsler, and learned, from high authority, that her saltations were more than poetry, where-upon he wrote the fragrant *Spanish Student*, which smells of the utmost South, and was a strange blossoming for the garden of Thomas Tracy.

In 1843 Longfellow bought the house. The two hundred acres of Andrew Craigie

had shrunken to eight. But the meadow-
land in front sloping to the river was
secured by the Poet, who thereby secured also the wide and winning prospect, the broad green reaches, and the
gentle Milton hills. And if, sitting in
the most midsummer moment of his life,
he yielded to the persuasions of the siren
landscape before him, and the vague
voices of the ancestral house, and
dreamed of a fate fairer than any Vassal,
or Tracy, or Craigie knew, even when
they mused upon the destiny of the
proudest son of their house,—was it a
dream too dear, a poem impossible?

In 1846 the *Belfry of Bruges* collection was published, in 1847 the *Evan-
geline*, in 1850 *Seaside and Fireside*, and
in 1851 the last and best of his works,
up to the present time—*The Golden
Legend.* In this poem he has obeyed
the highest humanity of the poet's calling, by revealing,—which alone the poet
can,—not coldly, but in the glowing and
affluent reality of life, this truth, that the

same human heart has throbbed in all
ages and under all circumstances, and
that the devotion of Love is for ever and
from the beginning the true salvation of
man. To this great and fundamental
value of the poem is added all the dra-
matic precision of the most accomplished
artist. The art is so subtly concealed
that it is not suspected. The rapid reader
exclaims, "Why! there is no modern
blood in this; it might have been ex-
humed in a cloister." Yes, and there is
the triumph of art. So entirely are the
intervening years annihilated that their
existence is not suspected. Taking us
by the hand, as Virgil Dante, the Poet
introduces us directly to the time he
chooses, and we are at once flushed and
warmed by the same glorious and eternal
heart which is also the light of our day.
This is the stroke which makes all times
and nations kin, and which, in any individual instance, certifies the poetic
power.

The library of the Poet is the long

northeastern room upon the lower floor. It opens upon the garden, which retains still the quaint devices of an antique design, harmonious with the house. The room is surrounded with handsome bookcases, and one stands also between two Corinthian columns at one end, which impart dignity and richness to the apartment. A little table by the northern window, looking upon the garden, is the usual seat of the Poet. A bust or two, the rich carvings of the cases, the spaciousness of the room, a leopard-skin lying upon the floor, and a few shelves of strictly literary curiosities, reveal not only the haunt of the elegant scholar and poet, but the favorite resort of the family circle. But the northern gloom of a New England winter is intolerant of this serene delight, this beautiful domesticity, and urges the inmates to the smaller room in front of the house communicating with the library, and the study of General Washington. This is still distinctively "the study," as the rear room is "the library." Books are here, and all the graceful detail of an elegant household, and upon the walls hang crayon portraits of Emerson, Sumner, and Hawthorne.

Emerging into the hall, the eyes of the enamoured visitor fall upon the massive old staircase with the clock upon the landing. Directly he hears a singing in his mind:

> Somewhat back from the village street,
> Stands the old-fashioned country seat,
> Across its antique portico
> Tall poplar-trees their shadows throw,
> And from its station in the hall
> An ancient timepiece says to all,
> > Forever—never!
> > Never—for ever!

But he does not see the particular clock of the poem, which stood upon another staircase in another quaint old mansion, —although the verse truly belongs to all old clocks in all old country-seats, just as the "Village Blacksmith" and his smithy are not alone the stalwart man and dingy shop under the "spreading chestnut tree" which the Professor daily passes upon his way to his college duties, but belong wherever a smithy stands. Through the meadows in front flows the placid Charles.

> River that in silence windest
>   Thro' the meadows, bright and free,
> Till at length thy rest thou findest
>   In the bosom of the sea !

So calmly, likewise, flows the Poet's life. No longer in his reveries can mingle more than the sweet melancholy of the old house's associations. No tradition records a ghost in those ghostly chambers. As if all sign of them should pass away, not only Mrs. Craigie's fellow-worms destroyed the elms in front, but a noble linden tree in the garden, faded as she failed, and languished into decay after her death. But the pensive grandeur of an old mansion sheds a softer than the " purple light " of the luck of Edenhall upon the Poet's fancies and his page.

EDWARD EVERETT

335

While we labor and while we rest, while we wake and while we sleep, God's chemistry, which we cannot see, goes on beneath the clods. Myriads and myriads of vital cells ferment with elemental life; germ and stalk, and leaf and flower, and silk and tassel, and grain and fruit, grow up from the common earth. The mowing machine and the reaper—mute rivals of human industry - perform their gladsome task. The well-filled wagon brings home the ripened treasures of the year. The bow of promise fulfilled spans the foreground of the picture, and the gracious covenant is redeemed, that while the earth remaineth, summer and winter, heat and cold, and day and night, and seed-time and harvest, shall not fail.

An Ideal Farm.

Edward Everett.

EDWARD EVERETT.

BY GEORGE S. HILLIARD.*

THE town of Dorchester, in which Mr. Everett was born, is one of the oldest of the Puritan settlements in Massachusetts Bay. It took its name from Dorchester, in England, where lived John White, a Puritan divine, who has sometimes been called "the father of the Massachusetts Colony" and "the patriarch of New England." The merchants who associated for trade in Massachusetts Bay in 1623 were from old Dorchester, and this town proved in the English rebellion to be one of the centres of opposition to

* Written in 1853 for Putnam's *Homes of American Authors.*

Charles the First. In his valuable paper
on the origin of Massachusetts, Mr. Haven has shown how close the connection
always remained between old Dorchester and the infant colony. Very naturally, the first settlers gave this familiar
and honored name to one of their first
and finest positions.

At the time of the siege of Boston
Dorchester attained some revolutionary
notoriety. The batteries thrown up by
Washington, which drove the English
fleet from the harbor in 1776, were established on Dorchester Heights. These
hills are within the present line of the
city of Boston.

The house in Dorchester in which Mr.
Edward Everett was born stands about a
mile from the centre of the village of
Dorchester, at a point long known as the
"Five Corners." Here Mr. Everett's
father lived from the year 1792, when he
left the charge of the new South Church,
in Boston, until his death in 1802.

We fear that no remarkable incidents

can be related of the history of this comfortable country residence. It is now occupied by Mr. Richardson, who has owned it for many years. After the death of his father, Mr. Everett's mother, with her young family, removed to Boston, and at the public school of Boston and at Exeter Academy he was fitted for Harvard College. He also attended in Boston a private school kept by the late Hon. Ezekiel Webster, the brother of Hon. Daniel Webster.

He entered college in 1807, at which time he was but a few months more than thirteen years old. He left college in 1811 the youngest member of his class, but with the highest honors of the college. His distinguished brother, Alexander, who graduated five years before, at the age of sixteen, was also the highest scholar in his class. Leaving the college halls which have been the homes of so many American authors, Mr. Everett in 1813 succeeded his friend Mr. Buckminster, the pastor of Brattle Street Church,

in Boston. His home was then established in the parsonage belonging to that
society.

It is not improper to say here that this
house, venerable from a half-antiquity,
although now surrounded by the noisiest
business of the city was appropriately
situated for the purposes of a parsonage
when Gov. Hancock presented it to
Brattle Street Church. The business of
the town has since swept all around it,
perhaps unfortunately for its occupants;
but, by the will of Gov. Hancock the
parsonage is anchored and is likely to
be, in that position. A house in which
Mr. Buckminster, Mr. Everett, Dr. Pal-
frey, and Mr. Lothrop have lived suc-
cessively, deserves mention among the
homes of American authors.

Mr. Everett left this residence when he
accepted the Eliot professorship of Greek
literature at Cambridge. He then spent
some years in foreign travel. When he
accepted the active duties of his professorship, he lived for some time in the

Washington house or Cragie house, the present residence of Prof. Longfellow. He afterwards occupied there a house in the pretty avenue known by students as Professors' Row. This house was built by Prof. Farrar, and is now his home.

Mr. Everett entered Congress in 1824, and was for ten successive years the representative of the Middlesex district. During this time the residence of his family, and his own while he was not occupied at Washington, was at first Winter Hill, in Charlestown, now in Somerville, —a place also noted in the history of the siege of Boston. He afterwards removed to the more thickly settled part of Charlestown, in Bow Street.

Mr. Everett was chosen Governor of Massachusetts in 1835. He was elected to this post for four successive years. During this time he resided in Boston, in the house which he now occupies, or at Watertown, in the house well known in that vicinity as the home for many years of the late Dr. Marshall Spring.

In the autumn of the year of 1839,—in
the delicately balanced politics of Massachusetts, where then, as now, parties
were very evenly divided,—and in a variety
of local questions which it would be hard
to explain in history or biography, Mr.
Everett received one vote too few, out of
more than a hundred thousand, and Gov.
Morton was elected his successor. There
is a good story told, of which we should
hardly venture to give the particulars, of
his describing this defeat the next year
to a European Grand Duke,—who listened to the precise statistics with no little curiosity. Grand Dukes have had a
chance since to learn the value of votes
better than they knew them then. In
the spring of 1840 Mr. Everett went to
Europe with his family. He spent a
winter in Florence ; and was engaged in
a summer tour, when he received his ap-
pointment as Minister to London from
the administration of Gen. Harrison.
He arrived in that city at the close
of the year 1841, and remained there

until he was recalled in the spring of 1845.

At this time the presidency of the University at Cambridge had just been vacated by Mr. Quincy's resignation. The friends of the University eagerly solicited Mr. Everett to become his successor. He accepted the invitation after some hesitation, and was formally inaugurated on the first of May, 1846. His administration of the University was short, but it is still gratefully remembered by those who were connected with it at that time. It inspirited and in some regards gave new tone to the venerable institution, — it certainly excited the enthusiasm of its friends,—and was signalized by some important enlargements of its endowments. The Lawrence Scientific School was endowed and established during these years. He was President of the University three years, when the condition of his health, which was not equal to the harassing requisitions of its thousand duties of detail, compelled him to retire.

A pleasant essay might be written by some Cambridge man, on that old "President's house," which Mr. Everett occupied while President, and for two or three years afterwards. It stands close on the high road, exposing its hospitable front to every blast of dust from roads dusty to a proverb. Magnificent in its day, it is, —though of old fashion and low ceiled rooms,—comfortable now. Its hospitalities never failed in the presidential dynasties which can be remembered ; and many a graduate and many a graduate's fairer friends, recollect the brilliancy of its lights of a Commencement evening, or as a "Class Day" celebration passed away ; the pleasant little retiring-places in its narrow grounds, and the spirited strains of evening music, from the performer hidden somewhere on such occasions in its shrubberies. And how faithfully remembered,—more distinctly, perhaps, than any of its rooms,—the wing in which was the President's "official residence." Here he administered rebuke or praise; and here passed those critical interviews of which the apocryphal narrations make so large part of the food with which witty Sophomore regales the craving ears of wondering Freshman.

For the present, all these associations are of the past. Dr. Sparks occupies his own house at some little distance from the college halls, and the old President's home is a lodging-house and boarding-house for students.

It was built in 1726–27. President Wadsworth,—whose name his descendant Professor Longfellow bears,—was its first occupant. Holyoke, Locke, and Langdon,—in the dynasty of the last of whom the college buildings were made barracks for the Revolutionary troops, whose successors, the students, were hardly less revolutionary : for he retired from· office when a body of impudent boys desired him to do so ;—Willard,— who planted the large trees around the house, and who is remembered by living students,—Dr. Webber, Dr. Kirkland, Mr. Quincy, and Mr. Everett have occupied it in succession. Here is our excuse for dwelling on its history among the Homes of American Authors.

Mr. Everett is again residing in his own house on Summer Street, in Boston. Many years since, this house was occupied by the Hon. Daniel Webster. Mr. Everett has recently added to it a beautiful library. The bookcases, which almost wholly surround the room, are of carved oak. No glass doors hinder the student. A single cabinet protects manuscripts and other private documents. It is lighted from above, and above the books there is, therefore, an excellent light for some fine pictures. Among those which hang in the room are portraits of Hon. P. C. Brooks; of Webster, by Healy and by Stuart; of Lord Brougham; of the Duke of Wellington and Sir Robert Peel; of Burke, and of John Quincy Adams. There are some curious antiquities and memorials of

Edward Everett

Mr. Everett's travels, in the room ; and
between the doors is stretched, a-couch-
ant, a beautiful marble hound, by Horatio
Greenough,—the quiet guardian of the
entrance.

———

The public career of Edward Everett,
while it evidences the thoroughness of
his culture, and the versatility of his
gifts, affords a remarkable illustration
of the demands of an enlightened republic upon her intellectual citizens. Instead
of proposing to himself a vocation accordant with his tastes, or an aim suggested by his peculiar ambition, the
nobly endowed son of a free and progressive commonwealth is led by the
force of circumstances and the instinct
of patriotism to dedicate his powers and
acquisitions to every form of mental
action and public service. The moment
his ability is known, it is appropriated in
whatever sphere the exigencies of the
time and community require. The utility

of his knowledge, the weight of his
character, his facility in affairs, and grace
of expression are claimed to vindicate,
sustain, or adorn the interests of his native land ; and, instead of a life-devotion
to individual pursuits, he is consecrated
to offices of great immediate value, with
little or no regard to the claims of his
personal genius. It is seldom that the
needful training, and the earnest will
combine in any one man so favorably as
to induce such a degree of excellence in
these varied functions, as to reflect permanent honor on the individual. Such,
however, is the case with Edward Everett. He has the rare merit of having
proved himself fully equal to the numerous and diverse relations he has fulfilled.
Other men of genius among us may be
represented by the scene their writings
have rendered famous ; his career is more
justly indicated by a view of his birthplace, which at once suggests a life of
mental activity and patriotic devotion,
and of the interior of the library where

the best hours of an honored maturity are passed, eloquent of that wealth of attainment and literary culture, which has been the source both of his extensive usefulness and wide renown. His birthplace is one of the memorable villages near Boston ; where may yet be seen the traces of dismantled fortifications, landmarks of the struggle for independence which nerved and elevated his ancestry, and prepared the way for those peaceful but hardly-won triumphs of the scholar, in which he has so largely shared.

At an early period, as before and subsequently, a peculiar local interest attached to the theological profession in Boston. An enthusiasm for eloquent and refined preaching obtained among the cultivated inhabitants. The Puritan morals and the respect for mental superiority which characterizes that community, together with the prevalence of a higher degree of literary taste, caused pulpit eloquence to be singularly appreciated. The list of Boston divines comprised the most honored names, and their social influence and position were remarkable. It is therefore not surprising that the friends of a new candidate for intellectual fame should urge him to adopt the ministerial vocation. In the case of Everett, however, a special motive for such a course existed. At the period when his talents and scholarship became known beyond the University ; a voice upon whose faintest accent the most intelligent congregation of Boston had hung with breathless delight, was hushed forever. Buckminster had closed a brief and beautiful life amid the tears of devoted parishioners ; and the vacancy thus created, Everett, also young, gifted, and without reproach, was urged to fill. Thus, at the very outset, were his abilities severely tested ; and it is proof enough of his superior mind, that so hazardous an experiment succeeded.

During the first year of his youthful ministry, and while enlisting the sympathies of a large and critical audience by his sermons, he wrote and published an able work on the intrinsic scriptural evidences of Christianity. It was, however, obvious to the disinterested admirers of Everett that his true field of action lay in the domain of general literature ; and that in promoting the interests of academic education, his taste and love of knowledge would find more ample results than in any exclusive pursuit. Accordingly, in 1815, when he attained his majority, he was elected Professor of the Greek language and literature in Harvard University, with leave of absence to prosecute his studies and recruit his health in Europe. He reached Liverpool at the critical moment when the intelligence of Napoleon's flight from Elba had thrown the whole continent into agitation ; and, therefore, lingered in England, until the battle of Waterloo. Thence he proceeded to Gottingen, and having acquired the German language, and made a tour of inquiry amid the seats of learning in that country, established himself, for a time, at Paris; and subsequently visited Scotland, Wales, different parts of France, Switzerland, and Italy, and passed the winter of 1818 at Rome. In the spring of the following year he made the tour of Greece, thence went to Constantinople, and returned to Paris and London by the way of Vienna. On his arrival in the United States, after four and a-half years of foreign travel and study, he commenced his duties as Greek professor—illustrating the language, history, and antiquities by an able and interesting course of lectures. As a contributor to the *North American Review*, which for some years was under his editorship, he became the most popular and effective exponent of American talent and culture which had appeared in the form of periodical literature. For ten years after relinquishing this genial and most useful department of labor, Mr. Everett was a member of the national House of Representatives. In 1835 he was elected Governor of Massachusetts, and held the office four successive years.

In 1841 he was appointed Minister to England; and, when a change of administration induced his return home, in 1846, he was chosen President of Harvard College. It is but a few years since he resigned that eminent office and took up his residence in Boston, where his time was divided between the literary avocations so accordant with his taste, and the pleasures of a cultivated society.

In the career thus outlined, we perceive all the elements desirable to give scope and inspiration to his rare gifts and systematic application. Each sphere in which he exerted his powers bore the fruits of genius, learning, and conscientious industry. Circumstances, too, were singularly propitious. With the solid though limited basis of New England morality and scholarship, and the impulse derived from a literary, social atmosphere, he entered upon the broad field of German culture, prepared to adopt its best and evade its baneful agencies.

Edward Everett

On his first visit to Paris, the companionship of Coray, who had so eminently promoted the Greek cause with his pen, put Mr. Everett at once upon a track of inquiry and feeling, which he afterwards nobly vindicated. In Rome he was intimate with Canova, and there studied ancient by the light of modern art. To Ali Pacha he carried letters from Lord Byron ; and no American scholar ever visited that classic region better prepared to realize its associations. The effect of these manifold advantages soon appeared. As a professor, while he unfolded the spirit of antiquity, he also prepared the most desirable manuals for the students ; and advocated the cause of modern Greece, in the pages of his *Review*, with a knowledge of the subject and an enthusiasm for liberty which won the unlettered, while it fascinated the learned. In Congress he united the most graceful oratory with a methodical and unwearied attention to the details of legislative business. As a foreign minis-

ter, the dignity and tact, as well as varied
acquisition, he carried into the social
circle, and his remarkable gift as an occasional speaker, gained for him universal
respect, and for his country peculiar
honor. As a critic, the good-natured yet
keen rebukes he administered to the
superficial commentators on our habits
and institutions, delighted thousands of
readers, and silenced the flippant horde
of travellers with a torrent of graceful
irony supported by facts and arguments.
As a man of letters, in every branch of
public service, and in society and private
life, Mr. Everett has combined the useful
with the ornamental, with a tact, a uni-
versality and a faithfulness almost unprecedented. At Windsor Castle we
find him fluently conversing with each
member of the diplomatic corps in their
vernacular tongue ; in Florence, addressing the Scientific Congress with characteristic grace and wisdom ; in London
entertaining the most gifted and wisely-
chosen party of artists, authors, and men

of rank or state, in a manner which elicits their best social sentiments ; at home, in the professor's chair, in the popular assembly, in the lyceum hall, or to celebrate an historical occasion,—giving expression to high sentiment or memorable fact with the finished style and thrilling emphasis of the accomplished orator; and, in the intervals of these employments, we find him sometimes weaving into beautiful verse the impressions derived from his observation or reading, as witness the "Dirge of Alaric and Santa Croce."

It has been said that Mr. Everett owes it to himself and his country to bequeath a memorial of his great acquisitions and brilliant endowments, more complete and individual than any which has yet appeared ; and it has also been confidently asserted that a portion of his leisure is dedicated to such an object. The best actual record of his industry and genius, however, exists in the volumes of *Orations and Speeches*, recently collected ; and we trust the public expectation that his critical and oratorical essays are to be thus gathered up, revised, and published, under his own eye, will be fulfilled.

If Webster is the Michael Angelo of American oratory, Everett is the Raphael. In the former's definition of eloquence, he recognizes its latent existence in the occasion as well as in the man and in the subject ; his own oratory is remarkable for grasping the bold and essential, for developing as it were, the anatomical basis—the very sinews and nerves of his subject ; while Everett instinctively catches and unfolds the grace of the occasion, whatever it be ; in his mind the sense of beauty is vivid, and nothing is more surprising in his oratory, than the ease and facility with which he seizes upon the redeeming associations of every topic, however far removed it may be from the legitimate domain of taste or scholarship. In addressing a Mercantile Library Association, he places

Commerce in so noble and captivating a light that the "weary honors of successful ambition," won by studious toil, grow dim in comparison with the wide relations, social influence, and princely munificence of the great merchant. He advocates the privileges, and describes the progress of Science, and the imagination expands in delightful visions of the ameliorating destinies of the world, and the infinite possibilities that crowd the path of undiscovered truth. He sets before an Association of Mechanics the relation of their pursuits to the welfare of man, and the importance of knowledge to the artisan, and their vocation rises at once to the highest dignity and promise. He enforces the natural charms and permanent utility of Agriculture, and the farmer's lot seems the most desirable of human occupations. The variety of occasions to which he has thus ably administered is the best proof of his fertile resources and adaptive power.

He has successfully plead for Greece

and Africa, for the prisoner and the in-
temperate, for art and literature, for
popular and college education, for rail-
roads and the militia, for the completion
of the monument on Bunker Hill, and
the restoration of York Minster, for
manufactures, trade, the distribution of
the Bible, and the cause of Ireland ; and

> From the eddies of oblivion's stream,
> Propitious snatched each memorable theme.

Equally impressive and graceful, while
the intellectual crowd, at a New England
academic festival, hang upon his familiar
accents, and when responding to the welcome of a foreign city ; and, crowned
with the graces of true oratory his eloquence is as unfaltering and appropriate
when uttered to a royal society as to a
delegation of Sacs and Foxes, and as
readily attunes itself to the fading memory of the illiterate old soldier, as to the
quick sympathies of the youthful scholar.

GEORGE BANCROFT.

Other governments are convulsed by innova-
tions and reforms. .   . . Our constitution,
fixed in the affections of the people, from whose
choice it has sprung, neutralizes the influence
of foreign principles, and fearlessly opens an
asylum to the virtuous, the unfortunate, and the
oppressed of every nation.

History of the United States.

362

GEORGE BANCROFT.

BY GEORGE W. GREENE.*

THE Indians called the finest of New England rivers, the Connecticut, River of Pines. The summer tourist to the White Mountains, ascending or descending its valley, finds little reason for the name remaining, until he reaches its upper shores, where occasional groves of pines remind him of the name and its significance. A broad, tranquil stream, it flows through much of the most characteristic scenery of the Northern States, from out the "crystal hills," from the shadow of Agiocochook, "throne

* Written in 1853 for Putnam's *Homes of American Authors.*

of the Great Spirit," as the Indians called
Mount Washington, dividing New Hampshire from Vermont,—the granite from
the green,—beneath graceful Ascutney
Mountain at Windsor, through wide
waving grain-fields, foaming over the
rocks in its sole important cascade at
Bellows Falls, then into a broader and
more open landscape as it crosses Massachusetts, making at Northampton its
famous bend—the Great Ox-bow. At
Springfield, the railways from every quarter meet upon its bankș, and its calm
breadth here, with the low, clustering
foliage of its shores, and the bold cliff of
Mount Tom glimmering in the hazy noon
gives tone to the day's impressions. The
traveller southward follows the stream
toward Hartford and New Haven ; the
northern traveller clings to its shore until
he reaches Northampton.

Lying in the heart of Massachusetts,
Northampton is one of the most beautiful of country towns. Looking over a
quiet and richly cultivated landscape, the

view from Mount Holyoke is of the same
quality as that from Richmond Hill, in
England. Gentle green hills, fair and
fertile meadows, watered by the River of
Pines. That river is not classic Thames,
and no grotesque Strawberry Hill nor historic Hampden Court, nor Pope's villa
at Twickenham, nor stately Bushy Park,
tell tales to the musing eye of the singularly artificial and amusing life which is
so strangely and intimately associated with
the graceful English scene. The River of
Pines laves its peaceful shores with Indian
lore. Terrible traditions of the fights of
the early settlers of New England haunt
the stream. Historic life in its neighborhood is not old enough to be artificial.
Like much of our pastoral scenery, which
seems the natural theatre of tranquil life
and a long Arcadian antiquity, the landscape of the Connecticut, so far as it is
suggestive, reminds the observer only of
the dull monotony of savage existence;
but,—irresistibly as the stream flows to
the sea,—bears imagination forward to

the history that shall be. Alone of all
scenery in the world, the American landscape points to the future. The best
charm of the European and Asian lies
much in its reference to the past. Human interest invests it all.

> The mountains look on Marathon,
> And Marathon looks on the sea.

But that sea is not only a sublime waste
of waters, with the inherent character of
every grand natural feature, but it teems
and sparkles all over with another spell.
And this charm is undeniable. The Pass
of Leonidas is more interesting than the
Notch of the White Mountains, because
man is the master of nature, and wherever human character has entwined itself with natural beauty, it becomes an
inseparable element of enjoyment in the
scene, and an element which enhances
the dignity of the landscape. Thus in
Concord, the spot upon the river's bank
where the battle was fought, is lovely
and tranquil, but how much lovelier—not
as water and foliage, but as feeling and

inspiration, which is the immortal beauty of landscape—for the remembrance of the human valor which consecrates it, and its significance and results.

No man, of course, grieves that American scenery is not generally invested with this character. Born upon this superb continent, heaped at intervals with the inarticulate mounds of extinct races, yet races which have left no historic trace, and can never be more than romantically interesting, we are fed upon the literature and history of the world. The grandeur of Egypt, the grace of Greece, the heroism of Rome, are all ours, and the lands illustrated by that various character do not fail to fascinate us. But at present our landscape is not unlike the Indian himself. It is grand but silent ; or eloquent only with speechless implication. Foreign critics complain that we are enamoured of foreign scenery, and do not know our own wealth. But our admiration for the old world is only our homage to that human genius which shall make our own story as splendid. Seeing what it has elsewhere done, we perceive no more truly what, in a sphere so stately and spacious, it will yet accomplish. A Greece more Greek and a more Roman Rome, is the possible future of America. Why are they so jealous of our delight in the Parthenon—in the Alps—in the Italian pictures? Shall we not honor the flowering of the power that ornamented the old lands and times, when we look to its future blossoming for our own glory? We prospectively honor ourselves in respecting the old world. And if, sometimes, the youth of a sensitive and delicate temperament, fully capable of enjoying to the utmost the resources of European life, and requiring the successes of art and the convenience of an old civilization for the happiest play of his powers, longs for the galleries, the societies, the historic shores, it may well be pardoned to him, in consideration that he is an indication of our capacity for that condition. He shows

what we shall be,—he shows that not
only the genius of creation, but of appreciation, is part of our constitution.

When, however, this peculiarity takes
the form of a querulous fastidiousness,
and, in Broadway, sighs for the Boule-
vards, and, remembering St. Peter's,
sneers at the Capitol, it is foolish and
offensive. But, on the other hand, we
shall not necessarily improve our nationality by perpetually visiting Niagara or
reading Mr. Schoolcraft's Legends, or refusing assent to the positive superiorities
of other countries and times. Essentially eclectic in our origin, we shall be
so in our development. Foreign critics
treat us as if we had not a common ancestry with them, but were descended
from the Indians. They say to us: " How
are you ever to have a nationality, if you
desert all your traditions and devote your-
selves to loving and imitating Europe?"
The question is fair, but the implication
is unjust. They forget, especially the
English critics, that our difference is not

absolute and final, but only relative.
We have the same history and language
with them. Their men and events are
peculiarly ours, more, that is, than Italian and Patagonian events and men, and
our literature, which they so obstreper-
ously insist must be national, necessarily
has a family likeness to their own. Many
of our books imitate English books just
as they imitate each other. The reason
is in the common language and the similarity of thought.

But no American need tremble lest the
grandeur of his country should fail to be
expressed in Art and Literature. Some
Homer, or poet along whose lines shall
flash and roar our boundless sea; some
Plato, or Catholic philosopher, in whose
calm wisdom the breadth of a continent
shall repose; some artist, who shall pas-
sionately dash upon immortal canvas the
fervor of our tropics, and realize in new
and unimagined grace the hints of forest
and prairie—these must all be, or the con-
ditions of human and national develop-

ment, as they appear in history, will not be fulfilled.

Certainly, looking from Holyoke, no man grieves that the Connecticut is not the classic Thames, nor that the Great Ox-bow is unadorned by Strawberry Hill. Nor do I suppose that he regrets upon the hill the absence of the dandies who composed the court of " the first gentleman in Europe," nor that of the Dutch royalty of his three predecessors. Fortunately for us, this law of association works both ways. Horace Walpole in the country, tormenting it with his fantastic fancies, is almost as incongruous a spectacle as Beau Nash by the seaside. But it is the glowing line of history in which these figures are insignificant that imparts the charm. The elegance of extreme refinement marks the pleasant view from Richmond Hill. It is akin in impression to that of the " lovely London ladies." It is in landscape what they are in society. But pastoral peace broods over the valley of the River of Pines.

Golden plenty waves in its meadows,—
the flowing tresses of a peasant. Gentle
mountains undulate around, covered
with green woods. A fresh sweetness
and virginal purity everywhere breathe
a benediction. If no historic heroism
inspires the mind of the spectator, there
is also no taint of sheer artificiality, none
of the nameless sadness which haunts the
gallery of King Charles's beauties. This
is Nell Gwynn, the ruddy orange-girl, her
youth and heart sweeter than the fruit
she bore ; not the painted and brocaded
lady, not the frail but faithful St. Albans.

Looking from the piazza of this house
at Round Hill, the eye grasps grim Monadnoc at the north, and the Yankee
hills of Connecticut, made poetic by distance. A tranquil and friendly landscape, somewhat lurid in our early history with Indian fires and desolations,—
a broad, fair river,—altogether a fine and
suggestive emblem of our constitution
and resources, it is pleasant to associate
with Northampton the commencement

of the work that records our history in a
manner which secures its final permanence. It is fortunate that it was written
now, while the outlines are not lost in
the mist of antiquity, and by one who,
to an original, clear, and profound perception of the great principles which appear in the development of the race, has
added the ripeness of rich scholarship,
long foreign residence, and that invaluable practical acquaintance with men
and affairs, which has made his own life
part of contemporary history. Best of all
for the purpose, the ineradicable Americanism of the historian imparts his native air to the page. It is not only a
History of America, it is an American
history. There is a wild vigor and luxuriant richness in its style of treatment, a
proud buoyancy of flow, as if it shared
the energetic career of the country it describes. The intellectual habit evident
throughout is precisely that required of
a historian, not so romantic as to limit
the story to a sweet and captivating le-

gend, nor so academic as to marshal in colorless masses the hosts of historic facts. It has no withered, scholastic air. The historian has not curiously culled flowers, and offered them to us pressed, —but with generous hands he gathers all the bounties of the field and heaps them before us, wet with morning dew.

Our present duty is not with the work, but with the cicumstances which the work has made interesting. Born near Worcester, Massachusetts, Mr. Bancroft was the son of the Rev. Aaron Bancroft, one of the most distinguished Unitarian divines of the last half century. In his house, the religion learned from his lips by his children was of that grave and humane catholicity which, once permeating the young mind, sweetens the man's life forever after. Freedom of inquiry, the supremest liberty of moral investigation, was the golden rule of the old man's life. "Prove all things," was the earnest exhortation of his preaching, sure that otherwise there would be little good to hold fast. When, in the declining years of his life, an intellectual and moral excitement, known as Transcendentalism, prevailed in New England, and many good men of his own persuasion fancied that the foundations of things were at last succumbing, the old clergyman went his way quite unperplexed, sympathized with the spirit, although not with the result of the investigation, and assured his alarmed friends that the errors, if such they were, would necessarily pass, and that all grains of truth grew in husks.

At seventeen years of age our historian went to Germany and studied at Gottingen. Like all ardent and serious New England youths, his interest in theological speculations was great, and he often preached to the quiet German country congregations around Gottingen, in their native tongue. This interest was the puritanical inheritance of his native land. The small towns were parishes, and the minister the high priest. It had been so

from the earliest times, and the feeling
in the matter, which survived until a
quarter of a century since, clearly manifested the fact that the emigration of the
pilgrims and the settlement of New England was a religious movement. Possibly,
seen from Gottingen, the theological traditions of New England might lose some
of their awful proportions. In the pleasant pulpits of Boston, the observer might
not always see the Cotton Mathers, and
other clerical Boanerges of the elder day,
nor trace in their limpid discourse the
fiery torrent of Puritan preaching. But
the spirit of inquiry inculcated by the
father, the pastor of the quiet country
town, was sure to preserve the inquirer
by neither exaggerating nor threatening.
The young man pursued his studies with
ardor, in every direction. His penetrating mind, contrasting the European
habit of education with our own, per-
ceived where ours failed, and what it was
necessary to do to elevate our standard
in the matter. Of singular intellectual

restlessness, his mind bounded and darted through the fields of scholastic culture, hiving the sweets, quite ignorant yet of their probable or final use.

During his residence in Germany, the young American student, bringing to the Savans of that country the homage of a fame they did not know to exist, was doubly welcome. In Berlin, he knew Schleiermacher, Wolffe, and Savigny. It was in Jena that he first saw Goethe. The old man was walking in his garden, in the morning, clad with German carelessness, in heavy loose coat and trowsers, without a waistcoat. He had the imperial presence that is preserved in all the statues and pictures, and talked pleasantly of many things as they strolled. Lord Byron was then at the height of his fame. Goethe asked of him with interest, and said, although without passion or ill-feeling, that the English poet had modelled his *Manfred* upon *Faust*. In this remark, however, Goethe showed more the pride of the author than the perception of the critic. For the theme attempted in both poems is precisely the one sure to fascinate all genius of a certain power, and the treatment in these special instances reveals all the differences of the men.

Afterward, in Italy, our student saw Lord Byron. He first met him on board of one of our national vessels lying at Leghorn, and to which the poet had been invited. As he mounted the side of the ship, Byron's eye fell upon a group of ladies, and he wavered a moment, saying afterward that he feared they were English, toward whom, at that time, he was not friendly. He advanced down the deck, however, glad to learn that the dreadful cloud of muslin enveloped nothing but Americans, and fell into animated conversation.

"Ah! Lord Byron," said one of the fairest of the group, "when I return to America no one will believe that I have actually seen you. I must carry them some tangible proof of my good fortune.

Will you give me the rose in your buttonhole?"

The "free and independent" address did not displease the poet, and he gave the rose.

Upon leaving the vessel, Lord Byron asked Mr. Bancroft to visit him at his villa, Montenero, near the city, to which, a day or two after, he went. They talked of many things, Lord Byron naturally asking endless questions of America. He denied the charge of Goethe about *Manfred*, and said that he had never read *Faust*. He had just written the letter upon Pope, and, in conversation, greatly extolled his poetry. Without saying brilliant or memorable things, Byron was a fluent and agreeable talker. It was in the year 1821, and he was writing *Don Juan*. "People call it immoral," said he, "and put *Roderick Random* in their libraries." So of Shelley, "They call him an infidel," said Lord Byron, "but he is more Christain than the whole of them." When the visitor rose to leave, the poet took down a volume containing the last cantos he had then written of the poem, and wrote his name in them, as a remembrance "from Noel Byron." But Ambrosia was that day allotted to the young American, for they had passed slowly through the saloon, the host bade him tarry a moment, and leaving the room immediately returned with the Countess Guiccioli. She, too, smiled, and gliding into the mazy music of Italian speech, led the listener on delighted. Again he rose to go, but a servant threw open a door and discovered a collation spread in the adjoining room. Perhaps the poet pleased himself with the fancy of graciously and profusely entertaining his foreign subjects in the ambassadorial person of his guest. "That is fame," he said, upon reading in some tourist's volume that a copy of the *English Bards and Scotch Reviewers* had been found by him at Niagara. The modesty of his American visitor might recognize in the cordiality of his reception and treatment Lord Byron's acknowledgment of his American fame.

In 1822 Mr. Bancroft returned home, and served for a year as Greek tutor in Harvard College. During his long residence in Europe he had matured his projects to raise the standard of education in America, and in the following year he, with Mr. Cogswell, now Librarian of the Astor Library, commenced the famous Round Hill School at Northampton. Three brothers Shepard, descendants of the old New England divine, had built three neighboring houses upon this spot. Gradually they had all passed into the hands of one of them, who was willing to sell them, and they became the seat of the school. The estate comprised about fifty acres. The school was immediately filled by young men from every part of the country, and took rank directly among the finest institutions. Mr. Bancroft devoted himself with unremitting ardor to the enterprise. The system of study pursued at the best schools in the world was introduced, and the scheme was, in itself, completely successful. Unhappily, however, there was no Oxford and no Cambridge for this Eton. The course of study was so high and entire that the graduates of Round Hill were well fitted to enter the advanced classes of any college. But, by a singular provision of College Laws, those who entered an advanced class were held to pay for the preceding years. Nor did the studies in any college carry the student forward to a proportional result. Shrewd men did not want to pay twice for their sons' education. Besides, it was a solitary effort,—possibly some wild whim, thought the shrewd men, of this deeply dyed German student. Thus, although in itself successful, it did not promise to achieve the desired result, like a very perfect blossom, which will yet not ripen into a fruit. Mr. Bancroft's interest in it, therefore, gradually declined.

Meanwhile, he had served other aims by translating his friend Heeren's *His-*

tory of Greece, and had been long meditating and preparing the material for a
history of the United States. In 1827
he was married at Springfield, and returning to Northampton resumed his connection with the school simply as a teacher.
He presently withdrew from it altogether
to write the first volume of his history
which was published in the year 1834.
The historian then removed to Springfield, where he resided two years, com-
pleting and publishing another volume
there.

It was a favorite maxim of Ariosto, and
of Lord Byron, that every man of letters
must mix in affairs, if he would secure a
profound influence upon men. Only by
contact, they felt, does man learn to
know man. The wandering Homer, the
actor Shakespeare, the statesman Milton,
Lord Bacon, the privy councillor Goethe,
Michael Angelo planning fortifications
for Florence, Leonardo da Vinci design-
ing drains for the Lombardy plains, are
names upon their side. It is easy to see

how invaluable to a historian must be this practical intercourse with men and affairs, of whose development history is the record. Mr. Bancroft's political career, therefore, is not only a remarkable illustration of the successes opened in a republic to ability and energy, but it has necessarily been of the profoundest influence upon his work. A man who makes part of the history of his own time, can better write that of another. While still resident at Northampton, he was, quite unwittingly upon his part, elected a representative to the General Court, but his engagements prevented his taking the seat. Other positions were offered him, which he declined. Appointed Collector of Boston, in 1838, by President Van Buren, Mr. Bancroft brought to his new duties an intelligence and zeal which secured the acknowledgment of great ability from very determined opponents. He was again married at this time his first wife having died the year before ; and, during the engrossing engagements of his office he labored diligently upon the third volume of the history, which was published in 1842. In the year 1844 he was nominated for governor by the democratic party. He was not elected, although receiving a larger vote than had ever before been polled upon a purely democratic issue. Party spirit did not spare any prominent man, and plenty of hard things were said during the contest. But in the excited moments of political difference, although great talent is often conceded to opponents, integrity and kindliness of heart are as often denied. Throughout a canvass of great acerbity of feeling, the democratic nominee was in New York, engaged in examining, often for more than the twelve hours of the day, the documents illustrative of our early history, which Mr. Brodhead had then just brought from Holland for the Historical Society of his state.

In 1844 Mr. Polk was elected President, and summoned Mr. Bancroft to Wash ington as Secretary of the Navy, and in the autumn of 1846 he crossed the ocean as Minister to England. When Rubens, the painter, resided in England as Dutch Ambassador, a company of diplomats one day called upon him and found him, pallette in hand, at work before his easel.

"Ah!" said they, "Monsieur the Ambassador is playing painter."

"No, gentlemen," responded the artist, "the painter is playing Ambassador."

So our historian played Ambassador, and played it well. Upon leaving Washington he said to the President that he should devote his energies to the modification of the Navigation Act, and his success in the effort is one of the chief triumphs of Mr. Bancroft's political career. He did not arrive as a stranger in London, but the scholars there, and the learned representatives of other countries, were already correspondents of the American scholar and loyal to the fame of the American historian. We have had no foreign representative more genuinely

George Bancroft

American. Still devoted to the aim of
his life,—by personal intercourse with
eminent men and close examination of all
material accessible in England, by constant correspondence with other parts of
Europe, especially France, and frequent
visits to Paris to explore its libraries and
search its archives, the *History of the
United States* went on. In 1849 Mr.
Bancroft returned to the United States,
and took up his residence in New York.
The fourth volume of the history, com-
prising the French war and the begin-
nings of revolution, was immediately
prepared for the press and published by
his old publishers, in Boston, in the
spring of 1852. Its success, after so long
and highly-wrought expectation, was entire, and confirmed the satisfaction that
the history of our country was to be
recorded by a mind so sagacious, so cognizant of the national ideas, so receptive
of the national spirit, so affluent of lore,
so moulded by intercourse and attrition
with great times and their greatest men,

so capable of expression at once rich, vigorous, and characteristic.

Mr. Bancroft's time is now divided between the city and the seaside. Early in the summer he repairs to Newport, and were the date of our book somewhat later, we might enrich our pages with an engraving of the house he is now building there. It will be a simple, summer retreat, lying upon the seaward slope of the cliff. From his windows he will look down upon the ocean, and as he breathes its air, impart its freshness and vigor to his pages. The fifth volume of the history is now printing. It will comprise the first events of the greatest epoch of modern times. Nor is it possible to say to how late a date the work will be continued. The great result of independence once achieved, the consequent organization of details can hardly be properly or copiously treated, until the mind can clearly trace the characteristic operation of principles through a somewhat longer course of years.

www.ingramcontent.com/pod-product-compliance
Lightning Source LLC
Chambersburg PA
CBHW021330110726
47900CB00005B/1416